Early Praise for
FAST FORWARD

"*Fast Forward* is a must-read for anybody interested in the evolution of digital TV, broadband, and streaming video. Craig Leddy's rich and deep industry research and knowledge is unparalleled."

—Bob Benya, former president and CEO, iN DEMAND, and VP and marketing, FSN

"*Fast Forward* should be on the reading list of all those interested in a better understanding of the digital distribution technology achievements that produced what we have today, as well as a primer on the dynamic processes involved in all cutting-edge development projects."

—Tom Feige, former division president, Time Warner Cable, and president, FSN

"What a story! Both the crazy project itself and the subsequent convergence of technology, media supply chain, content creation, user consumption behaviors, etc., etc."

—John Callahan, streaming software and product development consultant, former software manager, FSN

"*Fast Forward* provides a fascinating and comprehensive overview of the evolution of television from a linear medium with severely constrained capacity to today's world of nearly infinite streaming video-on-demand. I found *Fast Forward* to be an accurate and spellbinding account. It weaves together technologies, personalities, successes, and failures in a very readable way and helps us understand the world that we now inhabit a bit better."

—Jim Chiddix, former CTO, Time Warner Cable

"Great read. Craig got it right. I know; I lived it. This is our history in an engaging, accessible, and inclusive look at what we all did to change the world. And it made me revisit yesterday with a smile. Hope it does that with every reader."

—Paul S. Maxwell, media trade founder and publisher

"*Fast Forward* provides an essential chronicle of the development of digital television, interactive media, and on-demand streaming. While head of NBC Cable, TiVo, and other companies, I witnessed how digital technology prompted many hyped-up, overly ambitious efforts to achieve significant market adoption. Craig Leddy identifies the criteria that spells the difference between success and failure, and he tells the story in an engaging and entertaining way."

—Tom Rogers, CNBC founder and former president and CEO of TiVo, Inc.

"*Fast Forward* is a gripping, expertly reported account of the origins of digital streaming—the seismic shift that would come to define the modern era. With a journalist's precision and the pacing of a thriller, Craig Leddy unpacks the tangled web of technology, business, and culture that gave rise to today's on-demand world. As a scholar of societal transformation, I found it both enlightening and indispensable—a rare book that informs, engages, and endures."

—Ben LeBoutillier, award-winning author of *Practical Advice for a Better World*

"As a fifty-plus-year cable television veteran, I saw this fascinating history play out firsthand. Craig has crafted a thoroughly enjoyable television history and a *very* relevant study for the future of television. This is a must-read for anybody who works in television, and, frankly, for anybody who has ever *watched* television!"

—Rick Howe, producer and host of *The Friday Fireside* and *Talk Back to Television*

"Finally, someone has captured the story of the Full Service Network, a pivotal point in the evolution of entertainment, the internet, and the World Wide Web! Without question, it was one of the highlights of my career. *Fast Forward* excellently captures the insane ambition, the pure audacity of its vision, and the sheer determination of the many people who contributed to its success. Many thanks to Craig for his telling of this amazing story."

—Ralph Brown, technology consultant, former CTO, CableLabs, former chief software architect, Time Warner Cable

"Craig has been around long enough to have 'been there, done that'—in this case from the very beginning. His observations and experiences match up with my own memories of what was going down. He captured it perfectly."

>—Lou Borrelli, CEO, National Content & Technology Cooperative (NCTC)

"Craig Leddy expertly chronicles the revolutionary journey of video streaming. As the former EVP of Distribution at HSN, where we launched the first twenty-four seven interactive cable shopping channel, I found Leddy's insights into the challenges and triumphs of this media evolution very compelling. His engaging storytelling and expert analysis offer rare insight into how cable transitioned to the digital future. *Fast Forward* is essential reading for anyone eager to understand the dynamic landscape of modern media. Buckle up for an exhilarating ride!"

>—Peter Ruben, former EVP of Distribution, HSN

Fast Forward:
The Birth of Video Streaming,
Media's Wild Child
by Craig Leddy

© Copyright 2025 Craig Leddy

ISBN 979-8-88824-866-9

All rights reserved. No part of this publication may be reproduced, stored in a retrieval system, or transmitted in any form or by any means—electronic, mechanical, photocopy, recording, or any other—except for brief quotations in printed reviews, without the prior written permission of the author.

Published by

köehlerbooks™

3705 Shore Drive
Virginia Beach, VA 23455
800-435-4811
www.koehlerbooks.com

FAST FORWARD

The Birth of Video Streaming,
Media's Wild Child

Craig Leddy

VIRGINIA BEACH
CAPE CHARLES

Dedicated to innovators everywhere—
past, present, and future.

TABLE OF CONTENTS

PREFACE:
    DIGITAL WARRIORS 1

CHAPTER 1:
    THE RACE BEGINS 12

CHAPTER 2:
    THE WHITE NOTEBOOK 29

CHAPTER 3:
    PILGRIMAGE 38

CHAPTER 4:
    UNDER SIEGE 48

CHAPTER 5:
    THE $2-BILLION MAN 54

CHAPTER 6:
    THE DIGERATI COMETH 61

CHAPTER 7:
    THE ORCHESTRA LEADER 69

CHAPTER 8:
    HOME OF THE TWENTY-FIRST CENTURY 77

CHAPTER 9:
    NONE OF THE TOYS SMOKED 87

CHAPTER 10:
    LAUNCH DAY AND THE OH JESUS SWITCH 100

CHAPTER 11:
    KEEPING UP WITH THE WILLARDS 117

CHAPTER 12:
    THE FEWEST CLICKS WINS 126

CHAPTER 13:
  TIPPING THE SCALE 130

CHAPTER 14:
  FLYING HORSE 135

CHAPTER 15:
  REQUIEM 149

CHAPTER 16:
  THE OFFSPRING 159

CHAPTER 17:
  FROM THE ASHES 167

CHAPTER 18:
  BLIND FAITH 178

CHAPTER 19:
  WHO LOST CHINA? 185

CHAPTER 20:
  THE LEGACY 198

CHAPTER 21:
  DOOM AND REDEMPTION 204

EPILOGUE 213

PREFACE
DIGITAL WARRIORS

"We will lead the telecommunications revolution by merging cable, telephone and computer technologies to enrich our customers' lives through greater choice, control and convenience."
—The Full Service Network mission statement

JIM LUDINGTON RACED AROUND THE Network Operations Center (NOC), anxiously checking on the video servers and disc vaults. The refrigerator-sized servers held the first movies ever digitized for video-on-demand delivery. Down the road from the NOC, a global corps of some 300 journalists, including me, were sitting in a Sheraton Hotel ballroom in Orlando, Florida, waiting to see his handiwork displayed on a giant projector screen. If all went according to plan, Ludington and his team of developers would show the world things they had never seen before. He was the lead engineer for an ambitious project, grandly named the Full Service Network, to create a digital telecommunications network capable of delivering all manner of interactive media services—long before anyone called them apps. The developers, nervously awaiting their fate, be it a career-boosting triumph or an embarrassing failure, included top hardware and software engineers from some of the biggest media and tech companies of the day. After two years of tortuous development, they would demonstrate, among other things, on-demand movie streaming years before anyone heard of Netflix and interactive shopping, back when Amazon was just the name of a river in South America. The ballroom stage was set for a live unveiling to prove that interactive services could be delivered to cable-connected TV sets that sat in millions of American living rooms, what was being heralded as interactive TV. But, with seemingly the whole world ready to see it, the network kept crashing, right up until the night before showtime.

Ludington, with a burly build, a thick head of brown hair, and a mustache, was equal parts construction foreman and cable television engineer. Starting in 1993, he oversaw the building of the FSN NOC (called *the knock*). One of his primary tasks was to mash together large, hot, expensive, and unproven networking equipment through what he called "brute force integration." As zero hour approached for the launch event, Ludington was exasperated by the network's instability.

"The network, everything, was running along, and all of a sudden, this thing would tumble for no reason. You can't find it in error logs; you can't find any reason why you just lost the world. Sunspots, bad karma. That was the explanation: bad karma," he told me later.

Ludington loved to build things and learn about the technologies that made television run. Due to his family upbringing, he was also intrigued by what went on the TV screen. Growing up north of New York City, his mom, Pat Ludington, was a producer of *The Howdy Doody Show*, an iconic 1950s kids' show starring a freckle-faced boy marionette. This was unique in the '50s. "Being a woman producer was pretty strong for her time," Jim said admiringly. His dad, Al, had a long career at ABC TV, which, along with CBS and NBC, was one of the whopping three channels that Americans watched. His father held a variety of roles, including working as a cameraman, a cartoonist, and a director of post-production. When ABC began running Sunday-night movies, he edited the films to satisfy network censors—no swear words or hints of impropriety.

Dad's career advice to young Jim was this: "Stay the hell out of the television business." So Jim followed his penchant for building, graduating from Colorado State University in 1982 with a bachelor of science in industrial construction management. By then, cable television was taking off. There were new satellite-delivered networks, such as HBO, Showtime, CNN, MTV, BET, and ESPN. Nearby, Denver was regarded as the cable capital. There, cable companies infused with an entrepreneurial spirit were working to disrupt the TV establishment dominated by the Big Three broadcast networks. Jim tried to follow his dad's advice but "like everyone in cable, somehow you stumble in."

Cable required new engineering disciplines to get TV signals into households. It required construction of sprawling cable systems—stringing wires, hanging amplifiers, trenching, and other cool stuff that a builder guy like Ludington loved. He took an entry-level position in the Construction Division of American Television and Communications (ATC), a Denver-based cable operator owned by Time Inc., the venerable magazine publisher and owner of HBO. Following in his parents' footsteps, Jim wanted to be part of the next generation of television. As the 1990s opened, the advent of digital technology became his big opportunity.

In 1989 ATC became part of the newly merged Time Inc. and Warner Communications, forming the world's largest media conglomerate. FSN was the brainchild of Time Warner, driven by its ambitious chairman and CEO, Jerry Levin (pronounced *la-vin*, like *begin*). A slight man with a mustache and bookish demeanor, Levin possessed a fanaticism for transformational technology, leading to the success of HBO's launch on satellite and later the failure of the AOL Time Warner merger. With FSN, he wanted to push digital capability to its ultimate threshold before media companies even knew where the starting point was.

In his off hours, Ludington enjoyed smoking a favorite selection in a cigar bar or scuba diving atop Technicolor-bright coral reefs. But those pursuits couldn't stop him from obsessing about the next big force that would transform television: digital. In those analog days, he was part of a growing army of engineers who realized that digital technology was about to change everything in media, entertainment, and telecommunications—as well as everything else in the world.

It was becoming clear that transforming analog TV into digital could revolutionize the medium. Using efficient digital streams opened the possibility of hundreds of more channels, clearer pictures and sound, and the potential to turn TV into an interactive and on-demand platform.

But why bother with TV, a device that was derided as the boob tube and its fans as couch potatoes? At the time, TV was king. The internet was in its infancy, and the majority of consumers were afraid to go near a computer keyboard. Television had evolved from snowy black-and-white pictures to color TV and bigger glass screens. By 1990, TVs were in 98 percent of US households, the average home with two sets, while personal computers were in only 15 percent, according to Nielsen Media Research and the US Census Bureau. More than half of the TV homes were connected to cable wires that, in theory, could provide two-way communications, creating the potential for interactive TV (ITV). The definition of interactive TV was constantly changing, but the FSN developers, having spent months reimagining the TV experience, were about to present their version.

Although it was uncertain how to implement digital technology, what consumers wanted, or what the costs would be, America's media moguls and largest cable, computer, and telephone companies embarked on a race to reinvent television. John Malone, the most influential media force of our time, announced plans to use digital compression to provide a 500 channel universe. Bill Gates, who'd conquered personal computers with Microsoft, aimed to do the same with television. The gigantic regional Bell telephone companies, the so-called telcos, which had been spun out of the divestiture of AT&T, plotted ways to get around regulatory restrictions and distribute video services. The race to conquer TV continues to this day, now joined by colossal companies, including Amazon, Apple, and Google, as they compete with Netflix, Hulu, and others for supremacy in video streaming, the latest chapter in television's evolution.

In the early 1990s, no company possessed the wealth of content that Time Warner had: Warner Bros. films, HBO, TV productions, home video, music recordings, books, and Time Life magazines. As Levin recognized, a digital delivery network could provide new ways to distribute and monetize that content. He set the FSN plan into motion and vowed that it was not a trial but an actual service deployment. He no doubt regretted those words later.

So the stars were aligned for Ludington to be named as employee number one at FSN, one of the most daring, expensive, crazy, and important projects in the history of television and interactive media. In Orlando, armed with vague marching orders, he faced sky-high expectations and naysayers lurking within his own company's ranks that wanted to get him fired. Although it ultimately was deemed a failure and now is largely forgotten, FSN provided key linchpins in the development of television from a medium of limited analog channels to the digital, interactive, and on-demand services today.

On a highly conceptual level, the FSN plan went something like this: Build a brand-new two-way digital communications network, and transform television as we know it. Invent video-on-demand, create interactive shopping and advertising, enable video games to be played remotely, and devise a new type of telephone service. The ultimate goal, implied though not publicly declared, was to position Time Warner as the supreme ruler of every media company with digital aspirations. The service would essentially be the internet, controlled by the biggest media company.

Years later, Ludington sat across from me on a wooden outdoor deck at an Orlando bar, smoking a cigar and talking about the project with a mix of pride and bemusement. "No one had any idea what this thing was going to be," Ludington said. He blew out a cloud of cigar smoke and stared through it. There were the triumphs, yes, but there were also the setbacks. There were the gargantuan amounts of money spent, of course. And the day movie streaming came to life. That feat was likened to the Wright brothers' first flight at Kitty Hawk. He blew out another smoke cloud and muttered, "No idea what was going to happen."

■ ▶ ▶▶

As a business journalist covering media and technology, I was lucky to have a front-row seat to many key developments in digital TV and interactive media, including key phases of the FSN project. More importantly, I met the people behind the scenes and followed their personal journeys for years. Those journeys started in the heady 1990s, a time of great promise, opportunity, and achievement. The early developers of digital TV, interactivity, and on-demand video comprise one of the most important generations in media's evolution. With digital, the world changed dramatically, and it transformed everyone's lives along with it. It also fueled media titan egos, vaporware hype, and mistakes that still get repeated by media and tech companies to this day.

Like Ludington and his colleagues, I grew up fascinated by television, including the medium itself and the business and technologies behind it. Growing up in Columbus, Ohio, I was raised on *The Mickey Mouse Club* and Saturday-morning cartoons. I watched wide-eyed as the Beatles played on *The Ed Sullivan Show* and Neil Armstrong walked on the moon. My love of TV spilled into my journalism career. As a reporter in Washington, DC, I covered local cable franchise processes, Federal Communications Commission proceedings, copyright issues, and the deregulation of cable by Congress in 1984. My two brothers pursued television career paths, Kevin as a leading executive for Time Warner Cable and Charter Communications and Bruce as a Hollywood writer and director of shows, including *Mad TV*. My wife Margaret worked for the National Association of Broadcasters and, in one of the most fun jobs in the history of broadcasting, served as publicist at WGN-TV in Chicago for Bozo the Clown, the star of America's longest running children's TV show. Our Thanksgiving family dinner discussions ranged from episodes of *Seinfeld* to MPEG-2 digital compression.

As a reporter for media trade publications, including *Electronic Media*, and then editor of *Cablevision* magazine, I witnessed television's growth through some of its most significant stages: the launch of satellite-delivered cable channels, including C-SPAN and The Discovery Channel; the program syndication market boom with Oprah Winfrey and popular game shows; and the advent of digital technology, broadband internet, and video streaming. My role enabled me to meet industry leaders and inventors, both the well-known and the unsung, who strived to take the medium to the next level. Wherever technology takes television next, tomorrow's innovators will be standing on the shoulders of those pioneers.

UPON HIS ARRIVAL, LUDINGTON'S FIRST task was to transform a large, empty space in the north side of Orlando into a NOC, the brains of the groundbreaking digital distribution system. To pull off the FSN project, Time Warner would need to assemble a team in Orlando—dozens of engineers, content creators, and technology partners. They would have to be hardworking, motivated, and forward-thinking individuals who could build the distribution system, create the applications, and learn about user preferences. Perhaps most importantly for the company, they would need to discover exactly what consumers would pay for.

To accomplish all that, the team would be using primitive digital technologies that are laughable by today's standards. The team's primary task was to invent the capability for VOD movies, but many of the key foundations didn't exist. First, VOD required that the developers could get films that were in a usable digitized format for streaming. While some Hollywood studios had started to digitize their films, initially none were willing to give them to FSN. For the developers, it was like being asked to build a gasoline-powered car without gasoline.

"Streaming was not yet a technology," said Yvette Kanouff (nee Gordon), an FSN software engineer and NOC supervisor who helped to invent the digital fundamentals for VOD and DVDs (digital video discs). "We had to create the network and mechanism for video streaming, including encoding, transport, receipt, and all of the software and hardware. Today video streaming is an expectation. Then it was a science project."

Building the world's first digital cable system required the use of unproven digital video formats and broadband delivery architecture. Software engineers would have to write nearly all of the necessary code from scratch. Content creators would have to conceive how consumers would engage in virtual shopping. The developers would need to figure out how to allow neighbors to play video games against each other across a wired network. To enable users to manage new on-demand and interactive services, they would have to create new graphic user interfaces and redesign the TV remote. And they'd have to devise a way for people to order pizzas using TV, which is about the only thing that people seem to remember about the project.

Since Levin believed that speed to market was crucial, they were supposed to prepare all of this for an initial rollout to 4,000 suburban Orlando homes in about one year. Then, as the company revealed in a Securities and Exchange Commission filing, the plan called for FSNs to be rolled out across the company's cable service areas at an initial estimated cost of $5 billion ($10.4 billion in today's dollars).

Ludington's NOC quickly filled with the team, some referring to them as digital warriors. For months, the team toiled through frustrations and breakthroughs. Watching over them was a corps of reporters, turning the project into what FSN President Tom Feige called a "fishbowl pressure cooker." Hovering over all the development was a nagging question: Would consumers interact with television? After well-publicized delays, the developers were finally ready to show off the interactive services during the launch event on the morning of December 14, 1994.

■ ▶ ▶▶

ON STAGE, THE LAUNCH PLAN called for Levin and Jim Chiddix, chief technology officer of Time Warner Cable, to use an FSN TV remote to start the service and demo the apps, displayed on a giant projector screen. Chiddix, bearded and articulate, was prone to wax rhapsodically about technology in a deep, melodious voice, sounding more like a sorcerer conjuring up magic than an engineer distributing TV signals. He had an unflappable faith in technology, but his faith was being severely tested.

"I was nervous as hell," he recalled. "I knew way too much about what was behind the curtain. We were leapfrogging technologies in several dimensions, which was risky. There was lots that could go wrong. And I was pushing the button seemingly in front of every journalist in the Western world."

Engineers devised some backups so that the two execs weren't going out on the tightrope without a net. Louis Williamson, a Time Warner Cable engineer who pioneered the use of fiber optics, wired the main network and a backup development network into an A/B switch box. The device became known as the *Oh Jesus Switch*.

During the presentation, another engineer, John Callahan, was hidden behind the stage set and wired into a network of headset microphones connecting the NOC, Chiddix, and others in the ballroom. If Callahan or other technicians saw that the main network was going down, their instructions were to yell, "Oh, Jesus!" into their mike. That was the signal to throw the switch. If the backup network failed, they would yell, "Do the dance!" and switch to a second backup system, a complete FSN demo on a laser disc. The press was to be informed if the demo was on disc, although that remained to be seen.

The launch event was carefully scripted so that the engineers knew exactly what was going to occur as Chiddix clicked through the services. They had no idea that Levin was going to go off script and take the remote from Chiddix so he could play with the VOD movies, right in front of the audience and on a network that could crash at any moment.

The live event would give everyone one shot—only one—to show that digital VOD and interactivity were viable. If FSN crashed on launch day, it would be the digital TV equivalent of those films of early unmanned rocket failures, the ones of rockets exploding on the launch pad in spectacular fashion or taking off and then making a U-turn straight into the ground. The concept of interactive TV would get tossed on the junkpile of flying cars, jet packs, and other futuristic flops.

I CRAMMED MYSELF INTO A seat with the other journalists in the ballroom. Many media outlets had preceded the event with stories that ridiculed Time Warner for launch delays and unfulfilled promises. While the stage setup and confident corporate PR handlers provided an authoritative air, nobody could have guessed the risks behind the scenes.

Levin and Chiddix took their seats in front of a widescreen TV while the audience watched on the giant projection screen. Levin heralded the moment "as an irreversible step across the threshold of change, a step away from the world as it is to what it will be."

Chiddix picked up the remote that would start the service. Fingers were crossed. Even some journalists like me didn't want to have traveled this far to see the network break down. Although, there was the diabolical knowledge that it would make for one helluva story. Which was a juicier headline: "Interactive Service Debuts" or "Interactive Service Crashes and Burns"?

Ludington and the team inside the NOC stared at the proceedings on monitors. This was the moment of truth for the engineers, these digital warriors. Maybe this would be a historic moment, or maybe it would all be forgotten. And maybe this was for the press or Wall Street, and maybe it was really about corporate strategies and media mogul egos. But it was also for them, for all that they had accomplished. For all the hours of work, the hope, the promise. If it would *just work*.

CHAPTER 1
THE RACE BEGINS

John Malone sparked a television revolution by embracing digital compression technology (photo courtesy of Barco Library, Syndeo Institute at The Cable Center).

EARLY ON A SUNNY MORNING in Anaheim, California, in December 1992, two years before the planned launch of Time Warner's FSN service, the quest for digital TV dominance was sparked. I emerged from a hotel room and stumbled toward the Anaheim Convention Center, my head foggy from a convention party the night before. The cavernous convention center was the site of the cable industry's annual Western Cable Show, a major gathering of cable company, network programming, and technology attendees.

I made my way to the press room, where we'd been told there would be a major technology announcement by John Malone, the head of Denver-based Tele-Communications Inc. (TCI), then the largest US cable company and today a part of Comcast Corporation.

As a business journalist and editor of *Cablevision*, an industry trade magazine, I was skeptical of any media company's grand pronouncements. I had a personal *hype meter* in my mind, a bullshit detector that triggered an alarm when companies were overselling some technological marvel. As I neared Malone's press conference, my hype meter was on overdrive.

The press room was packed with reporters, cameras, and hot lights. The crowd spilled into the hallway, where I strained to catch a glimpse of Malone.

The square-jawed Malone was the cable industry's shrewdest executive, having built TCI into a cable giant through guile and clever financial maneuvers. At various points in his astoundingly influential fifty-plus-year career, Malone could lay claim to being the largest owner of cable systems in the United States, Europe, and Latin America. He was also the largest owner of satellite TV as the onetime chairman of DIRECTV. As head of Liberty Media Corp and its subsidiaries, his portfolio of partially or fully owned properties has included dozens of cable channels, a 27 percent chunk of Charter Communications, and once the Atlanta Braves baseball team. More recently it has included SiriusXM Radio, Live Nation, and Formula 1 motorsports. Malone also became the largest owner of private land in America, with property holdings estimated at three times the size of Rhode Island. Yet for all his wealth and notoriety, former coworkers noted that he led an unpretentious lifestyle, even driving the same car for years.

Depending on which side of the negotiating table you were on, Malone was either a brilliant visionary or a sly villain. In his book *Cable Cowboy: John Malone and the Rise of the Modern Cable Business*, author Mark Robichaux recounts how Malone built TCI through financial tactics that always kept him a step ahead of his creditors. During cable conventions, onlookers hung on Malone's every word, trying to predict the chess master's next move. *Why is he saying that? Who's going to benefit? Who's he going to destroy?* He'd been called Darth Vader and the leader of the cable Cosa Nostra—and those invectives didn't come from rivals or jilted partners. They came from members of the US Congress, primarily then-Senator Al Gore Jr.

Congress, largely at the urging of Gore in response to a wave of anticable fervor, delivered a serious blow to the cable industry by re-regulating it through the 1992 Cable Television Consumer Protection and Competition Act. Prompted by cable's transgressions for poor customer service, the act reeled in the industry that had been deregulated in 1984. Cable had been infiltrated by some entrepreneurs who appeared to be more interested in acquiring customers than caring for them. With many cable systems, there was no such thing as 24/7 customer service; on the weekends, all the employees went home so there was nobody to answer the phone. Across the country there was a persistent complaint from consumers: "My cable's out, again." Cable operators, who previously were heralded for fostering more choice in television versus broadcast TV, were portrayed as greedy monopolists. To this day, cable operators argue that municipalities created the problem by imposing unrealistic construction schedules and demanding expensive public amenities, from TV production trucks to tree planting.

Through the Cable Act, Congress heaped on regulations, including price controls on basic cable unless a cable system could prove that it faced "effective competition." President George H.W. Bush vetoed the Cable Act, but Congress overrode him, the one and only time that Bush was overridden in his entire presidency—because of the cable industry.

Meanwhile, the FCC authorized the launch of satellite TV to compete with cable while the Bell telephone companies—the telcos—made moves to get into TV distribution. Cable operators worried about the coming of DIRECTV, often referred to as the Death Star, and the formidable phone giants. As editor of *Cablevision* magazine, it was clear to me that the cable industry was in trouble. Someone or something needed to save the industry.

Congress had taken its best punch against cable, and now Malone was about to show that it left no marks. (He once told *The New York Times*, "I have no respect for politicians, and I'm very poor at suppressing that.") With that backdrop, the likely purpose of the TCI press conference was for Malone to prove that cable wasn't going to disappear and, in the process, figuratively raise his middle finger to the federal lawmakers who were 3,000 miles to the east.

At first, Malone's announcement seemed technical and unexceptional. TCI was joining forces with General Instrument, the leading manufacturer of cable set-top boxes and networking equipment, to embrace emerging digital compression technology. From a technical standpoint, that meant that TCI was going to add more cable TV channels by using a digital video format instead of the traditional technique of analog radio frequency (RF) signals. *So what?* I wasn't impressed.

But, gradually, the implications became clear. By applying an emerging digital compression format known as MPEG (*M-peg*, Moving Picture Experts Group), a cable system could pack more channels—eight, ten, or perhaps even twelve channels—into the same bandwidth space as one single analog channel. At best, an analog cable system could deliver about fifty to sixty TV channels. If a cable system could multiply its current channel lineup by a factor of eight, ten, or twelve channels, then it meant that the cable system could vastly expand the television programming that it offered to customers. Additionally, transforming analog video into a digital stream of bits would produce clearer TV images and sound. Malone suggested that the digital format could promote a new world of more pay-per-view options and special programming to serve audience niches.

The next morning, a *Wall Street Journal* headline spelled it out in different terms: "Need More TV? TCI May Offer 500 Channels."

From that point on, Malone was credited with coining the phrase "the 500-channel universe," an enduring mantra of the industry. But, as he chuckled later in an oral history for The Cable Center, he never really used that term. TCI's announcement, Malone recalled, "hit headlines as 'Malone says five hundred channels' and all of that. But the arithmetic is pretty easy. If cable systems have got fifty analog channels, and you can do ten-to-one compression, that wasn't a huge leap of mathematics."

After the press conference, cable technologists were abuzz about what Malone's digital transformation could mean. Not only were more channels in the offing but perhaps other dreamed-of services: interactive program guides, on-demand movies, instant information and data communications (whatever that meant back then), perhaps even telephone service. In the 1970s and 1980s, cable companies promised these "blue sky" services in order to win municipal franchises. Few of those promises were ever met. Now there was an even bluer sky to offer.

But going all digital would require a technological sea change of unfathomable proportions. Cable companies would have to lay more fiber-optic cable and install new equipment to distribute digital signals. They would have to install new digital set-top boxes in every customer home to provide digital TV channels. Hollywood would have to digitize its movies while TV shows, news, sports—everything—would have to be converted or produced using digital formats. There were variations in the specs for MPEG, modulation, and other technical requirements and little consensus between industries or companies. The broadcasting industry and consumer electronics manufacturers were entrenched in debates over competing video and audio specifications for high-definition TV. In short, there were a lot of moving parts but few ways to connect them.

So my question after Malone's announcement was this: Is this just hype or an actual harbinger of bigger things? During a reception that evening in the Anaheim Marriott's Orange County Ballroom, amid long tables topped by bowls of shrimp and colorful assortments of veggies and cheese, I asked Fred Dawson, one of the industry's veteran technology writers.

"The cable industry usually goes along like this," he said, gesturing a gradual series of ascending steps. "Then something comes along and it goes like this." His hand turned more vertically. "Now the industry just went like this." His hand shot straight upward like a rocket.

Malone's announcement generated welcome attention for the beleaguered cable industry and sent TCI's stock price up 10 percent. *The Los Angeles Times* said, "No. 1 Cable Operator Will Switch to Digital Technology: The new compressed signal system will make possible a huge increase in the number of available channels and pave the way for a variety of advanced TV services." *The Washington Post* ran a front-page story: "TV's Brave New World: 500 Cable Channels on Video Horizon."

To some observers, the idea of 500 channels seemed ridiculous, when most cable systems had a few dozen channels and there still was "57 Channels (And Nothin' On)," as Bruce Springsteen sang in 1992. Who needed 500 channels, and what in the world would fill them all? A *New York Times* headline said, "A Cable Vision (or Nightmare): 500 Channels." *Washington Post* writer Paul Farhi wrote, "The Age of Video Overload is at Hand." Comedians joked about the potential for wacky new networks like The Poodle Channel. Although, some ideas that initially seemed absurd, like Golf Channel, became billion-dollar enterprises.

Whether it was hype or not, other companies weren't going to stand by and let Malone be the flag-bearer of the Digital Age. Word started circulating of other digital schemes, whether real or merely designed to impress investors.

Inside Time Warner, Jim Ludington's bosses scoffed at Malone's plan.

■ ▶ ▶▶

IN THE 1990s, TIME WARNER'S headquarter offices were located at 75 Rockefeller Center in Midtown Manhattan, several hundred feet from Rockefeller Center, with its sunken ice rink and eighteen-foot-tall cast bronze statue of the Greek Titan Prometheus. Bare-chested and hovering above vertical water fountains, Prometheus's gigantic left hand appeared to be reaching toward the street, past a stainless-steel relief on the front of what then was the Associated Press Building, artist Isamu Noguchi's ode to journalists of a bygone era. The bronze god seemed to be gesturing toward the Time Warner building at the end of the street, the gateway to traditional and new media, fronted by a charcoal-black entryway with three golden revolving doors.

Those golden doors constantly turned through both media prosperity and market turmoil. They served as carnival wheels to a Time Warner executive's fortune or their professional doom. The thirty-three-story building was the center of the world's largest colossus of media properties: movies, TV, cable, home video, music, books, and magazines. But that boastful measurement of corporate superiority would be of little consequence to the gigantic Prometheus, because he was doing something beyond any business executive's capacity. In his right hand, he brought fire to mankind. Carved in the red granite wall behind him were these words: Prometheus, Teacher In Every Art, Brought The Fire That Hath Proved To Mortals A Means To Mighty Ends.

Inside the Time Warner building, behind the black façade and golden doors, Jerry Levin, Time Warner's chairman and CEO, sought to create a new form of fire: interactive media. For Levin, interactive media was akin to a religious calling.

Raised in suburban Philadelphia, Levin's father ran a butter and eggs business, and his mother was a piano teacher. His upbringing was marked by biblical studies at Haverford College that led him to question his Jewish heritage, leaving him "very spiritual, but a-religious," as he told *BusinessWeek*. Perhaps instead of worshiping a higher power, he became passionate about transformational technology and the capacity of media to enrich lives on earth.

As head of HBO, he witnessed the power of transformational technology by beaming the pay-TV service off satellites in 1975. This was a watershed event that made HBO a powerhouse and inspired the launch of hundreds of satellite-delivered cable networks. Levin's fanaticism for technology and interactive media attracted both admirers and skeptics. Later it would ignite outright scorn when he and then AOL Chairman and CEO Steve Case joined together to create AOL Time Warner in 2000. It was the biggest merger failure in US history.

Jerry Levin was a fervent believer in transformational technology (photo courtesy of Barco Library, Syndeo Institute at The Cable Center).

Despite his seemingly mild manner, Levin demonstrated a steely resolve and high ambitions, having dispatched his chief rival in order to become head of the company. He was anxious to get going with the FSN plan. Recognizing that other cable, computer, and telephone companies had similar aspirations, he was hell-bent on being first to market. "Sooner isn't only better; it's often everything," he proclaimed.

At the time of Malone's announcement, Time Warner was going

through one of the lowest points in its history. Steve Ross, the flashy chief executive who'd assembled the media conglomerate, died of cancer in December 1992. Public sentiment about the company and Levin, who'd taken control of the CEO post over Nicholas J. Nicholas, Jr., were grim. *New York Newsday* said, "The vision that created Time Warner has died with Ross. The only reason there is a Time Warner is that he wanted things that way. Now that he's gone, so is the rationale for Time Warner."

In terms of personality, Malone and his Denver cohorts were the near opposite of Levin and his Eastern elite. Malone, while heading cable equipment manufacturer Jerrold, had turned down a job offer from Steve Ross, instead joining with Bob Magness, a former Texas rancher who started TCI. Like some other Western cable companies, TCI was populated by former builders and pole climbers who approached the business with a construction mentality because, after all, cable, in many respects, was a construction business. Time Warner, as a media company, was more focused on the programming and services that cable had to offer. Levin and Time Warner were suit and tie; the Westerners were open collar and jeans. Malone was John Wayne, and Levin was Peter O'Toole in *Goodbye, Mr. Chips*.

TCI and Time Warner Cable didn't compete directly against each other because they operated in separate cable franchise areas. In the collegial cable business, the two companies often worked together and with other cable companies to support technology development and achieve goals for the industry's common good. But the corporate leaders had competing visions of how to embrace digital. When it came to the prospect of global domination, collegiality only went so far.

Before TCI's announcement, Time Warner was experimenting with fiber-optic cable and determining how servers, switches, and computing capability could transform a cable system into a digital dynamo. A week after the Western Show, the company's initial thinking about the FSN plan surfaced during a Paine Webber media conference.

"Some MSO [multiple system operator] executives last week

downplayed the hoopla over TCI's scheme to deliver 500-plus channels," *Multichannel News* reported. "Time Warner senior vice president Geoffrey Holmes responded that his company is taking a 'more expansive' approach toward new technology by focusing most heavily on building high-capacity fiber networks rather than signal compression.

"TCI's plan will primarily benefit the MSO's pay-per-view business, Holmes said, but doesn't do enough to develop new businesses or even the core business. 'What we're trying to do is to build a new network that can offer us a large variety of revenue streams, as opposed to just pay-per-view,' Holmes said. 'When you look at what John [Malone's] doing—and we will be doing some of that as well—what you're talking about is an interim step in terms of where the network architecture is going to go.'"

FROM HIS PERCH AS CHIEF technology officer of Time Warner Cable (TWC), Jim Chiddix had been watching the incoming forces of the digital revolution swirl around him. It was his next chapter in a lifelong fascination with technology.

Growing up in Easton, Pennsylvania, the son of a research chemist, Chiddix took interest in such boyhood pursuits as microscopes, chemistry sets, and model trains. He went to Cornell University to study electrical engineering but detoured into the Army. He eventually taught electronics at the Air Defense Command School in El Paso, Texas, focusing on systems designed to calculate the trajectory of incoming missiles so they could be stopped in their tracks. He finished at Cornell, worked on computers, and bounced around until he ended up in Hawaii. There, he sailed and worked for an early cable system on the outskirts of Oahu that offered a grand total of six TV channels.

He joined Oceanic Cablevision, a Hawaiian cable system owned by Time Inc.'s ATC, that became a test bed for new technologies, including pioneering the use of fiber optics to transmit video content. Among ATC's ranks were Joe Collins, Carl Rossetti, and Louis Williamson, each of whom would play a key role in FSN. When Time and Warner merged, the combination of ATC and Warner Cable gave Chiddix and his fellow engineers a bigger sandbox to play in.

Jim Chiddix recognized how digital could dramatically transform cable service (photo courtesy of Barco Library, Syndeo Institute at The Cable Center).

After progressing to TWC's Stamford, CT, headquarters, sandwiched between I-95 and Long Island Sound, Chiddix and his colleagues saw how the prospects for digital technology were evolving. With digital, a cable system could be transformed from a clunky retransmitter of analog channels into a robust, interactive network. Fiber-optic cable, which is made of glass strands to transmit using light waves, could vastly increase capacity. Running a lot of fiber lines was cost prohibitive, but they could be combined with lower cost coaxial connections to the home in what ATC dubbed hybrid fiber-coaxial architecture (HFC). The two-way services that cable had been promising franchising authorities since the late 1970s, and that were largely untenable using analog technology, could become a reality with digital.

New silicon microprocessor chips were taking computer capability and image processing to higher levels, and that would constantly improve. Chiddix was fond of quoting Moore's law, named after Intel cofounder Gordon Moore, who showed that computer processing power doubles every two years. While performance doubles, costs remain the same, meaning you get twice as much bang for your buck.

The potential for providing interactive media was getting recognized in many quarters of the cable, computer, and telephone industries. At the time, it seemed to make sense to focus on TV as the delivery mechanism. TV sets were in nearly every US household, and more than half were connected to cable that could provide the means for interactivity with the click of a TV remote. The internet was taking hold with academics, government departments, businesses, and computer geeks but had yet to become widely viewed as a vehicle for home entertainment. Home computers were big boxy things supported by DOS instruction manuals that practically required a computer science degree to understand.

Why waste time and money trying to turn geeky computers into interactive entertainment vessels when the TV set was right there in the living room? All you needed to do was make it smarter. Even Bill Gates saw the opportunity and sought to turn the TV into an interactive device, powered by Microsoft technology, of course.

The concept of interactive TV had been dreamed about for years. On December 1, 1977, Warner Cable, then headed by Gus Hauser, launched QUBE in Columbus, Ohio, the first two-way interactive cable system. Although it relied upon analog technology, QUBE enabled local cable customers to respond to poll questions displayed on TV. It helped spawn pay-per-view movies, music videos (The Monkees band member Michael Nesmith was involved), and channels that were predecessors to MTV and Nickelodeon. QUBE helped Warner to win urban cable franchises across the country.

Other cable franchise bidders promised all manner of blue-sky services: polling, banking, education, and "data communications"—whatever that meant then. The promise of cable and potential for interactivity energized the industry and attracted fresh investment, leading American Express to become a partner in Warner Communications, Getty Oil to invest in ESPN, and publisher McGraw-Hill to partner with TCI in Express Information Services. Express was essentially a newswire service for PCs, headed by longtime cable trade publisher Paul Maxwell.

The idea of merging cable's distribution network and computer capability blossomed as convergence became the latest industry buzzword. In 1985 Tom Wheeler, who, along with Jim Mooney, led the National Cable Television Association (since renamed NCTA—The Internet & Television Association) effort to deregulate cable, left the association to head NABU Network. It was a computer network designed to run on cable systems and provide personal computing, games, on-demand news, home banking, and other services, including a baseball app that predated fantasy sports.

Like so many early digital projects, NABU's aspirations were ahead of technology's capability. "We had to build our own computer," Wheeler said in an oral history for The Cable Center. "This was days of Commodore 64s and T1 [phone lines that provide top data speeds of only 1.5 megabits per second]. Real primitive operations . . . We couldn't sell it. We couldn't refinance it. The whole thing cratered." In 2013 President Obama appointed Wheeler as chairman of the FCC, where he led the effort to institute net neutrality rules that were strongly opposed by the cable industry that he had helped to deregulate.

As digital capability was blossoming, ITV services came back into play, and, whether real or not, they could be used for business advantage. Time Inc. and Warner Communications had merged in 1989, largely so that Steve Ross and co-CEO Dick Munro could thwart an effort by Paramount CEO Martin Davis to buy Time. The $18-billion merger left Time Warner with a hefty debt load. Needing a financial boost, Ross searched for potential investment partners, including some of the biggest tech companies of the day: IBM, Xerox, and Toshiba.

To convince new investors, Ross, a master showman, needed to demonstrate that Time Warner was part of a new age, not yesterday's news. The answer wasn't with the Time Inc. magazines or the Warner Bros. movie studio; it was with the cable systems and their potential to distribute more channels and new services. A series of presentations was lined up for the master showman to work his magic.

"So I was part of the dog and pony show," Chiddix recalled in an interview for The Cable Center. "I was the guy who got up and sort of gave the technology story."

During a rehearsal in the Time Warner building for one of the big pitches, Chiddix began his story about how fiber optics was transforming cable into a communications network with the potential for interactivity and the capability to provide 1 gigahertz (GHz) of bandwidth. Cable systems measure their bandwidth—the amount of electronic spectrum that they can devote to running TV channels and other services—in terms of megahertz (MHz) and gigahertz (GHz). A 1 GHz cable system would have about twice the bandwidth capacity of most cable systems back then. (These mega and giga figures shouldn't be confused with megabits-per-second (Mbps) and gigabits-per-second (Gbps) numbers that are used to measure internet speed.)

For the Chiddix rehearsal, Levin and Joe Collins, chairman and CEO of TWC, were present, along with Ross, who began to listen very intently. As Chiddix was presenting, Ross stopped him.

"Now, let me get this straight. You mean this technology exists today?" Ross wanted to know. "This fiber stuff? You could really do this and deliver a gigahertz of services?"

"Well, the technologies exist," Chiddix said, giving an appropriately theoretical engineering answer.

"Well, by George, we're going to do this," Ross declared. "You go out and build this in one of our cable systems."

And then he said the fateful words, "Don't worry about the money."

Chiddix smiled over the memory. "I could see Joe Collins next to me sort of turning pale because he knew that giving a blank check to an engineer was a very bad idea, potentially a very expensive idea, but this was the chairman of the company, and he wasn't going to have any argument about this. This was something important for us to do strategically."

Later, Levin told me, "We came up with the phrase 'Full Service Network' as part of that presentation. We were trying to have nomenclature for cable, which even at that time was called CATV, to get cable positioned so that the plant could deliver not just more TV channels but lots of telecommunications and interactive services."

So, who came up with name 'Full Service Network' first? Memories are a bit hazy. (The name currently is being used by a telecom company in Pennsylvania.)

"I'll take credit for the name Home Box Office," Levin said. "But I believe we came up with it as part of this presentation—Dennis Patrick, Chiddix, Geoff Holmes. It was helpful because FSN became a branded thing."

In a portion of its New York City service area in Queens, Time Warner launched the predecessor to FSN, a cable system called Quantum using 1 GHz of bandwidth. Although it was all analog, because digital hadn't come of age, Quantum offered 150 channels, including 60 channels of pay-per-view (PPV) with access to movies starting at multiple start times. Ludington was a principal engineer for the Quantum project. The cable division's VP of marketing was Hugh Panero, who later headed PPV service Request TV and then became president and CEO of XM Satellite Radio.

With traditional PPV, viewers could purchase and watch a movie only at a set start time. John Sie, a visionary marketer and technologist who worked for Malone, is credited with coining the PPV term. Later he said he regretted that it instilled the word "pay" in consumers' minds. Sie was a pioneering advocate for interactive cable, HDTV, and subscription video-on-demand (SVOD), and he became founder and chairman of Starz Entertainment Group.

By offering a movie at more starting times, the new PPV approach became known as near-video-on-demand (NVOD). While Time Warner was testing the concept in Queens, TCI was taking a similar approach in the Chicago suburb of Mt. Prospect, IL, offering start times of a movie every fifteen minutes. TCI was rumored to have a room full of young people racing around on roller skates and popping videocassettes into VCRs at various start times, although former executives said that was more of a joke than reality.

With Quantum, Ludington recalled, "You could order a movie, and we started them every fifteen minutes. So we had racks and racks of VCRs that had the same movie eight, nine times because each one was starting in fifteen minutes—or ten minutes or thirty minutes, depending on the popularity of the movie." But Ludington and his colleagues knew that NVOD wasn't going to win the digital race.

NVOD is like near beer—it's not the real thing, and it lacks any punch. NVOD wasn't digital, nor could it really be considered a technological breakthrough. NVOD just whet the appetite for a much bigger idea—being able to access a movie or TV show whenever you want and use your TV remote to manage full-motion video: play, pause, rewind, Fast Forward. True video-on-demand.

AT TIME WARNER AND IN other quarters, engineers started to recognize how digitized video could be delivered in a stream that could be manipulated. Using a video server in the central network office—called a headend in cable parlance—connected to a client device in the home—a cable set-top box—true VOD would match the capability of a VCR without the VCR. No more driving to the video store, where some stores would charge a fee if you returned a movie late or forgot to rewind it. Many rental videocassettes were emblazoned with a sticker that read, "Be kind, please rewind."

Sizing up the situation at the time, Ludington said, "So now you,

Time Warner Cable, have one hundred and fifty channels, and then TCI said, 'We'll have five hundred channels.' So the digitizing was starting to go on with what's in the pipe; then our next step was to prove that true interactivity works. No more store and forward. We're gonna do true two-way communications over our cable network. That was one big piece of the puzzle. So streaming goes on top of that—setting up a stream. That included all the things that were invented in that period of time. That's why I look at stuff on YouTube and everything else today, where they're setting up these individual sessions of video streaming to an individual device. Guess what? That was all done through FSN for the first time on the planet."

The Quantum trial inspired Levin to move forward with grander ambitions. Now he had his eye on VOD, ITV, and perhaps even phone service, which cable companies had coveted for years. Levin wanted to move to what he called "the ultimate phase." Other companies were thinking about the digital equivalent of a mission to orbit the Earth; Levin wanted a moonshot. Inside Time Warner, some weren't as optimistic and suggested more modest steps: perhaps a limited VOD R&D project, a kiosk that would demonstrate interactivity, or a trial of PCs in a local area network (LAN) that would imitate the internet.

The Quantum project required manufacturers to develop 1 GHz amplifiers, new set-top boxes, and other components that had never been attempted before. The equipment was developed fairly quickly, and the Quantum trial was launched with relative ease. That result, Chiddix said, was both a blessing and a curse, because the company was "feeling flush about Queens" and wasn't realizing how much more difficult it would be to provide a full-motion VOD network.

In his deep, melodic voice, Chiddix said, "Like many technologies that people can understand conceptually, the actual implementation of a widescale deployment takes much longer."

CHAPTER 2
THE WHITE NOTEBOOK

Time Warner presented reporters with a white notebook that outlined the ambitious FSN plan (photo by Craig Leddy).

Eight weeks after Malone's announcement, I was invited to attend a Time Warner press briefing on the morning of January 26, 1993, at the Time and Life Building in Manhattan. The company billed it as "a background briefing session on technological developments in our industry."

The press briefing was scheduled to last four hours. What could possibly be important enough to warrant holding reporters for four hours? In today's world of instant news, you'd be lucky to keep reporters' attention for a half hour.

As the press arrived, we were handed a white loose-leaf notebook with "Full Service Network" printed on the cover. Inside, a press release announced, "Time Warner to Build First Full Service Network; the Electronic Superhighway into the Home." It went on to say, "The network will be operational for demonstration by the end of the year with service available for residential customers [in Orlando] in early 1994."

The briefing's length was due to Jerry Levin's desire to accomplish so much. This was his moment and the company's opportunity to stake their claim in the digital future. Levin had gathered top executives of Time Warner divisions to show that they were united as one big family and would use digital to leverage their assets and transform every part of American media and telecommunications. The reporters sat in rows, watching Levin at center stage, a scene that would be repeated in 1995 with Time Warner's merger of Ted Turner's Turner Broadcasting System, and again in 2000 with the AOL merger.

Together these media titans would unveil a grand plan, bigger than Malone's idea or anything being ballyhooed by anyone else. To back up their assertions, the FSN notebook contained detailed schematics of network architecture and service plans that would leave reporters impressed or confused. Either was fine by Time Warner, as long as they got the message that this was a big fucking deal.

Levin's fascination with transformational technology wasn't just a grandiose CEO fantasy. He'd witnessed what it can achieve. By guiding HBO onto satellites, starting with a live broadcast of the *Thrilla in Manila* boxing match between Muhammad Ali and Joe Frazier in September 1975, HBO became the very definition of *cable*. Hotels and motels across the country put signs out front promoting that they had HBO.

Satellite delivery ushered in the modern age of cable. It sparked the imaginations of a generation of people who previously had no real prospects in television:

- Ted Turner, a loudmouthed yachtsman, bounced a small Atlanta UHF TV station off a satellite to create a nationwide superstation, TBS, and then in 1980 launched CNN, the first twenty-four-hour news channel.
- John Hendricks, a member of the University of Maryland faculty, read about the HBO launch in *The New York Times* and was inspired to start The Discovery Channel.
- Gerry Laybourne, a woman interested in media and child education, saw the potential for a new form of children's programming and cofounded Nickelodeon.
- Kay Koplovitz, who'd written a master's thesis on satellite communications and coordinated press coverage of the HBO satellite launch event in Vero Beach, FL, founded USA Network.
- Bob Johnson started Black Entertainment Television (BET), Brian Lamb put the House of Representatives on TV via C-SPAN, televangelist Pat Robertson birthed the Christian Broadcasting Network (CBN), and Bill Rasmussen and other sports fans delivered ESPN from the small town of Bristol, CT.

Young Americans were sold on "I want my MTV!" Municipalities awarded cable franchises to wire their communities for this new phenomenon. For a generation of business and technology professionals, cable fulfilled an appetite for a post-hippie era attraction to free speech, self-expression, and entrepreneurial spirit.

In a 2015 interview to mark the anniversary of the satellite feat, Levin, then age seventy-six, told me the two high points of his professional life were the launch of HBO and the launch of FSN.

■ ▶ ▶▶

As the reporters waited for a promised light buffet lunch, Levin laid out a broad vision for "the Digital World," as he called it. The company had cut its teeth on the Quantum project, "our fiber-rich highway into neighborhoods," he said. Time Warner would compress its TV signals, but, in a dismissive nod toward Malone's 500-channel plan, the company was "not entering a channel sweepstakes."

Under the FSN plan, all information would be digitized and delivered through high-speed data packet switching to "form a magnificent star-switched system." I thought that sounded cool, whatever it meant. Adding computer capability, FSN would serve up "movies on chips" for multiple viewing access. The amount of information into the home would be infinite. "This is the electronics superhighway of the twenty-first century," Levin declared.

Gesturing toward his division chiefs, Levin said the plan was not a cable-only strategy but a corporate-wide strategy that required all of the divisions' input. Levin eschewed the word "synergy," an overused business term applied to company mergers; he preferred to call it "combining resources." For Time Warner, 40 percent of its cash flow came from the cable operator division while 60 percent came from copyrighted "stuff"—movies, TV programs, magazines, books, and music—that would increase in value as it was resold through different interactive and on-demand formats, he explained.

One after another, division executives stood before the audience of reporters and voiced their support. Chiddix outlined the fiber architecture; Bob Zitter, HBO's top technologist, discussed digital compression; Joe Collins reported on the Orlando system upgrade; Dennis Patrick, a former FCC chairman who headed the company's telecommunications business, offered telephony and mobile opportunities; and Geoff Holmes presented multimedia service plans. The lone woman in the group, Terry Hershey, president of Warner New Media, brought a content focus from Burbank, CA. But the

Warner Bros. film studio and home video unit were conspicuously absent, for reasons that would become clearer later.

My notes from the event show how the advent of digital produced thinking that was all over the map, with statements that proved to be prescient, wrong, or just plain odd. Levin predicted that the on-demand capability would make the notion of channels obsolete. This was a cutting-edge concept later pushed by Apple, Google, and other companies that didn't really understand television. Hershey suggested fanciful interactive features, including programming the cable system to force-tune a person's horoscope and biorhythms for the day, instantly accessing how-to books taken to video, conducting financial transactions through TV, and viewing a model in a size-six sweater, having her turn 360 degrees, and then enabling consumers to purchase the clothing. (This concept later morphed into an overused interactive TV notion of buying Jennifer Aniston's sweater while watching *Friends*). For some unknown reason, HBO's Zitter, one of the smartest technologists in the business, said, "I don't know why anyone needs HDTV." (Zitter and HBO later became leaders in HDTV.) In another swipe at Malone, Collins said the TCI plan would create only a NVOD experience while Time Warner's plan for instant-start on-demand movies was "the real McCoy."

Among other ambitious plans, the promised FSN telephone services—before cable systems had any capability to offer telephone—included alternative access long-distance service to bypass local phone companies; personal communications service (PCS), a type of mobile telephone; business video conferencing; and picture phone, "offering full motion video of the parties displayed on a standard television screen." Distance learning was listed; proponents of new services usually sought to show that there was an educational benefit. There was no mention of the internet, but the plans included high-speed local area networks (LANs) for business data. The technical schematics mentioned a "broadband switch," long before the term broadband became synonymous with high-speed internet service.

At the time, video games were already a huge business, but they were based upon cassettes or CD-ROMs; nobody had figured out how to play games across a network yet. Time Warner's Atari had pioneered video games, although the unit was riding a roller coaster of financial ups and downs. A list of planned FSN services included video games that "are accessed by the customer from central digital storage and can be played with any other user in the system. Eventually, the games will be full-motion video and three-dimensional."

During questioning from the reporters, Levin predicted that hooking up homes for FSN, including the computer-infused set-top boxes that would connect to TVs and deliver a powerful graphics interface, initially would cost the company about $900 each—"not high enough to extinguish the business," he quipped, eliciting laughs from the other Time Warner executives. It's unlikely that they were still laughing when they learned the boxes alone cost more than five times that amount.

Throughout the proceedings, we, the reporters, attempted to process the overload of information, wrestling with a queasy mixture of fascination and skepticism. For some, their hype meters were clattering like Geiger counters in a uranium mine. Given the grandiose scope of the project, it's surprising that no one jumped up and exclaimed, "Are you *kidding*?" Perhaps it was the notable skepticism or a lack of excitement in the air that led Levin to push the envelope further. He uttered words that would come back to haunt him: "This is not a test."

Wow, everyone thought, *Levin is all in*. The CEO even doubled down by casting the FSN announcement as a "statement to the creative community" that Time Warner was creating "a perfect medium, because we have a highway into every home." He acknowledged that Time Warner had lost $20 million in the 1980s—ironically, in Orlando—on an experiment with teletext, a primitive form of delivering text-based news and other information on television. But now the company possessed the capability and the content library to go ahead and build the ultimate interactive network. "I don't want to wait for the twenty-first century," he said. The company would go out and build the future now.

And what would all of this cost? The FSN announcement began an industry guessing game that still goes on today. Estimates of the total cost run from the hundreds of millions into the billions. Some hints of the true cost were revealed as the project wound down in 1997. But as far as the potential commitment to a broad rollout of FSNs, Levin indeed was all in. Time Warner's 10K annual report filed at the end of 1993 stated the company's plan to "upgrade a significant percentage of cable systems to FSN capacity over the next five years at an estimated cost of $5 billion." One billion of the cost of capital expenditures was to be funded through a $2.5-billion partnership investment in Time Warner Entertainment by US West. US West was a Regional Bell operating companies that was seeking a slice of the interactive TV pie.

THE FSN ANNOUNCEMENT GENERATED WIDESPREAD publicity, although it received much less coverage than Malone's news, having come in the shadow of the 500-channel reports. Some of the most positive reactions were in the international press. Tammy Lindsay (now Tammy Snook Quezada), FSN's VP of communications and media spokesperson, said the foreign press was always fascinated with FSN. *The Financial Times* of London called FSN "the most ambitious interactive cable-based home entertainment and communications network yet attempted in the US on a commercial basis."

In the US, some newspapers picked up a perfunctory Associated Press account by Skip Wollenberg with a posed photo of Levin gesturing toward a large FSN schematic with the words "Electronic Superhighway" on it. Levin, with his dapper business suit and mustache, looked like either a university economics professor or a 1920s industrialist. Judging by the placement given to the AP article, some newspaper editors regarded the story more as filler for empty page space in Sunday editions rather than breaking news that heralded the future of television.

Internally, Levin achieved a personal goal, one that had as much to do with the future of Time Warner as his own professional survival. He had made an effort to unite the disparate divisions behind a common mission, even though it would test their level of enthusiasm. If he could oust Nick Nicholas, there was no guarantee that others wouldn't oust him. In Hollywood, Warner Bros. studio leaders Terry Semel and Bob Daly were frequently at odds with New York corporate while Warren Leiberfarb, president of Warner Home Video, resisted anything that could derail the division's home video revenue, according to sources and books about Time Warner. A few blocks away from Time Warner headquarters in New York, Michael Fuchs had brandished his star as the brash, ambitious head of HBO. With a quick internal coup, the revolving golden doors of the Time Warner building could spin out Levin and leave him flat on his ass.

The press conference projected Levin's leadership and was a step toward showing that Time Warner was one company. Looking back, Ed Adler, the company's VP of corporate communications, said, "After spending a long time trying to define Time Warner, we were on to something that could."

Despite considerable skepticism that Time Warner could pull it off, other companies hastily put digital strategies into motion. The stakes were too high to ignore.

Over the next few months, word surfaced of new interactive projects. Bell Atlantic, one of seven Regional Bell spinoffs that sought to compete with cable, planned a VOD service called Stargazer. Viacom, which, in those days, owned cable systems as well as program networks, planned an interactive TV trial, dubbed Advanced Interactive Consumer Video Services, with AT&T Technologies in Castro Valley, CA. GTE, then the largest independent phone company, tested an interactive service called mainStreet in Cerritos, CA. IBM, the biggest computer giant of the day, sought to marry computer and cable capability into a multimedia service, according to *Cablevision* magazine.

Other big players joined in. Sega, the giant video game company, created a cable-delivered Sega Channel interactive game service for its Genesis consoles. Discovery Communications founder John Hendricks began developing a TV service called Your Choice TV, offering on-demand, time-shifted TV shows. Barry Diller, the former head of Fox Inc., acquired QVC, the home shopping channel, "to propel him to the forefront of cable TV's technological revolution," as the *Los Angeles Times* reported.

In addition to cable's largest technology suppliers, General Instrument and Scientific-Atlanta, technology companies across the spectrum of computers, consumer electronics, and telecommunications jockeyed for position in the interactive TV competition. The companies seeking to supply technologies (listed in order of their interest level in ITV, in my opinion) included Microsoft, IBM, AT&T Technologies, Toshiba, Oracle, Sony, Intel, Sun Microsystems, Hewlett-Packard, Zenith Electronics, Hitachi, Pioneer, and Digital Equipment Corporation. Apple occasionally was mentioned as a prospective player in ITV, but it headed off on its own revolutionary, world-conquering journey with Macs, iPods, iTunes, iPads, and eventually iPhones.

As *Time* magazine noted, by 1993 Americans were spending $12 billion annually on home video rentals, $4 billion on video games, $65 billion on residential phone service, and $70 billion on catalog shopping. Using an interactive network, somebody was going to take a big chunk of those businesses. At that point, it wasn't a widely accepted notion that the winners would use the internet. But those in the know in Silicon Valley were licking their chops.

CHAPTER 3
PILGRIMAGE

FSN developers Mike LaJoie, Louis Williamson, and Jim Ludington played key roles in television advancements (photo courtesy of Laura Nolte, former FSN marketing manager).

> Those who dare to fail miserably can achieve greatly.
> —John F. Kennedy

A TENNIS BALL SLAMMING OFF a wall inside an empty building makes a really cool sound. Jim Ludington repeatedly propelled the yellow ball into the clean white walls with his large hand. Ludington struck an imposing presence as he played handball alone in the cavernous space, the air thick with the smell of fresh-cut sawdust and new paint. Sweat dripped down Ludington's forehead, and he soaked through his long-sleeve white dress shirt and black polyester pants. He reached up and ripped off the multiprint tie that was part of the business dress code imposed by the local cable system management, which repeatedly tried to get him fired.

As force met mass, fueled by a considerable dose of anger, Ludington smashed the tennis ball into the wall with great velocity, the sound echoing off the walls and linoleum floor like submarine sonar resounding in a vast ocean. His makeshift handball court was supposed to be getting transformed into a Network Operations Center that would usher in the future of television. But there were so many issues, delays, and arguments. Maybe if he hit the ball hard enough, it would break through all of the barriers standing in his way and knock some sense into the thick skulls of the naysayers inside his own company.

On a speakerphone lying on the floor near his crumpled tie, a conference call was raging. The speaker crackled as hardware engineers from companies in Denver and Atlanta argued with software engineers in Silicon Valley, leaving Ludington caught in the crossfire in Orlando. Ludington had muted his phone so nobody could hear him playing handball. The call droned on for hours. The engineers argued over server sizes, storage requirements, operating systems, software formats, interactive applications, delivery timelines, and, ultimately, who was in charge.

Oh jeez, thought Ludington, *next they'll be arguing over the color of the sky*. How were they supposed to revolutionize television if nobody could agree on anything? Ludington unmuted his phone.

"Hey!" he interrupted. "I'm the one who has to build this. I'm the one who has to rack and stack all the equipment. I'm the one who has to make all the wired interconnections and figure out how to power all this stuff and meet the cooling requirements. If you're gonna bring in ten, twelve, fifteen, twenty of these things for X amount of storage for X amount of movies, then I gotta find the floor space and the cooling and electric and fit it all. How are we gonna house all this stuff? How are we gonna integrate it all? How are we gonna make all this *work*?"

There was a long, empty silence on the other end of the line. A couple drops of Ludington's sweat ran off his forehead and dripped onto the speakerphone as he waited for an answer. Then the hardware and software engineers went back to arguing with each other. Ludington jabbed the mute button, swore, and picked the tennis ball back up.

Since Time Warner had declared a revolution, now it was up to Ludington to be the flag bearer. He had to build the FSN NOC and prepare to install equipment that had untested power and cooling requirements. Somehow, all the components—video servers, disk vaults, network switches, signal modulators, and in-home communications terminals—would have to be combined into a seamless interactive network through the brute force integration that Ludington foresaw.

There was so much work to do. Ludington knew the digital tsunami was coming, even though nobody could have predicted the magnitude. But until the engineers arrived in Orlando, the software code was written, and the equipment was built for this newfangled interactive cable system, he might as well play handball in the empty building.

TELEVISION BECAME A PHENOMENON IN the post-World War II 1940s and a fixture in US homes in the 1950s, providing a new source of entertainment and information and bringing viewers closer to the world. Times were different, however. TV journalist Edward R. Murrow smoked cigarettes while conducting interviews, and Americans thought it was particularly funny when comedian Milton Berle wore a woman's dress. American culture and TV culture became intertwined, steeped in Walter Cronkite, *TV Guide*, and Swanson TV dinners. With the advent of color TV, the medium evolved into a "carousel of color," as the popular Sunday-night show *Walt Disney's*

Wonderful World of Color heralded in its theme song.

Cable TV came along and disrupted the broadcasting establishment, offering more channels and outlets for creativity. In addition to the originators of new programming networks, cable required bold entrepreneurs to take on the enormous task of wiring America, stringing coaxial cable to poles, trenching through cities, and connecting homes. The story of the early cable entrepreneurs represents one of the most remarkable chapters in US business history. They took the promise of television to new heights and laid the foundation for the internet. Like the early network programmers, they came from diverse walks of life. Among the many forerunners who became part of industry lore are the following:

- John Walson, an appliance shop owner in Mahanoy City, PA, erected an antenna on a mountaintop in 1948 to retransmit Philadelphia broadcast TV stations over coaxial cable so buyers of TV sets had something to watch. The practice became known as community antenna television (CATV), and Walson's idea started Service Electric, regarded as the first cable system.
- Ralph Roberts, a former belt and suspenders salesman, entered cable in 1963 by acquiring a small system in Tupelo, MS, the beginning of Comcast.
- Chuck Dolan founded Manhattan Cable TV and, in 1972, launched a pay TV channel that was acquired by Time Inc. and renamed by Levin as Home Box Office, HBO.
- Bob Rosencrans used his UA-Columbia Cablevision system in Florida to carry Levin's HBO satellite launch and was the first to write a check for Brian Lamb's C-SPAN as a public service.
- Glenn Jones drove around in a Volkswagen bug pitching limited partnerships to build the MSO Jones Intercable, which also pioneered satellite-delivered radio and distance learning through Mind Extension University.

- Bill Daniels, a former US Navy World War II fighter pilot, was an outgoing Denver entrepreneur and onetime Colorado gubernatorial candidate who expounded about professional ethics and was instrumental in attracting capital for cable companies, earning him a title bestowed by NCTA as the father of cable television.

- Amos Hostetter got an MBA from Harvard Business School and then met Daniels, inspiring a partner and him to invest $3,000 for Ohio cable systems that were the start of Boston-based Continental Cablevision.

- Alan Gerry, from Liberty, NY, who studied electronics while a US marine, founded Liberty Video, originally focused on selling TV sets until he discovered the larger opportunity of providing cable service and created Cablevision Industries.

- Rocco Commisso, an Italian immigrant who'd served as chief financial officer for Gerry's company, founded Mediacom Communications, one of the last independently owned private cable companies. His name is on an Upper Manhattan soccer stadium where Columbia University plays, and he owns the Italian football club ACF Fiorentina.

The cable pioneers connected TV to homes, and now digital technology would open incredible new opportunities. Every generation of technology produces innovators that capitalize on the opportunities before them. Broadcasting produced the builders of America's first TV stations and program networks. Cable pushed the premise by offering new TV choices. With digital, the one-way transmission pipe for TV signals could be transformed into a two-way conduit to provide far more channels and interactive services. Early on, there were various predictions of what the world would become. But nobody could have guessed what would really happen.

■ ▶ ▶▶

WHILE LUDINGTON TOILED TO BRING digital to life, the Orlando communities around him were in an analog slumber. Nearby were suburban neighborhoods with pastoral names like Sweetwater, Wekiva Springs, and Spring Valley that had sprouted around man-made lakes near the Maitland exit off Interstate 4. These communities sit about a half-hour drive from the spectacles of Disney World, Universal Studios Florida, and Orlando's other monstrous tourist attractions. A huge tourist industry had been built from alligator-infested swamps.

For several decades, people in Orlando lived like the rest of the country. They read newspapers in the morning, sent mail through the post office, talked on landline telephones with long, curly cords, and watched a handful of existing TV channels.

By 1990, new forms of media and cultural experiences were introduced, albeit in an analog mode. Back then, you might have seen women jogging in bright polyester exercise suits and fluorescent-colored Nikes while listening to Garth Brooks on yellow Sony Sports Walkman cassette players. Kids played Super Mario Brothers on Game Boy handheld gadgets that were popular yet primitive compared to the gaming devices to come. Families videotaped gatherings by lugging around bulky black camcorders. For weekend entertainment, a family could rent a movie on VHS tape and play it on their videocassette recorder, although that meant driving down to the local Blockbuster video store. Once there, you could easily be out of luck if all the copies of a particular movie were already rented out.

Today it's hard to comprehend how different things were in the predigital era. TV was delivered to you on each channel's times and terms. Cell phones had limited network coverage and were nearly the size of a brick. Internet services hadn't taken hold yet. It was before America Online (launch date 1991), Amazon (1994), Yahoo (1995),

Google (1997), Facebook (2004), YouTube (2005), and Twitter (2006). Nobody called anything an app or took a selfie.

There were no iPods, iPhones, or iPads. No smartphones, smart TVs, or smart anything. Streaming, searching, and sharing weren't done electronically. People didn't text, tweet, emoji, Snapchat, or Instagram. You couldn't ask Siri or Alexa, hail an Uber, floss dance on TikTok, or get lost by Waze. No OMG, LOL, or FOMO. In 1990, Facebook cofounder Mark Zuckerberg was in kindergarten.

The digital wave was coming, and the Orlando suburbs were destined to feel some of the first ripples. About 4,000 lucky homes were slated to be connected to FSN and become the first households on the globe to experience what interactive media truly could do.

Ludington's empty NOC gradually filled with personnel and technology to deliver the digital wonders. History was about to be rewritten, change was in the air, and the Interactive Age was at hand. TV viewers would no longer be subjected to mindless reruns of *Gilligan's Island* or Lawrence Welk's bubbly champagne music. They wouldn't be merely "grazing" on TV channels, an industry term that likened viewers to cows. They would be transformed into thinking, breathing prospectors of instant information, consumable products, and on-demand gratification. Interactive TV offered a new mantra for television: choice, convenience, and control. Those who would provide this miracle of modern technology would reap billions of dollars. As the wonders of interactivity were about to take hold, the FSN developers, those digital warriors, headed to Orlando to join Ludington as the vanguard of a new age.

If it worked.

■ ▶ ▶▶

DAY AFTER DAY, NEW RECRUITS arrived in Orlando to support the project. Kanouff left a job with a US military defense contractor because FSN "seemed like a lot more fun than working on missiles."

Growing up in California, Mike LaJoie, who would tackle FSN's apps development, was a kid with a natural fascination: "If it whirred, clicked, buzzed, spun, blinked, I wanted to know why." Bob Benya, a hotshot marketer, arrived from a cable operation in Sweden and immediately found himself in charge of constructing a Home of the 21st Century to showcase FSN services and home electronics.

Daniel Levy once worked in video production for the NBA Entertainment, creating programming such as the sports documentary *Michael Jordan: Come Fly With Me*. Hal Wolf and Robert Montgomery came from Home Shopping Network, and Rick Colletto brought a laid-back vibe from Hawaii. After a series of culture clashes between Silicon Valley, cable, and telecom managers, Time Warner brought in Tom Feige, a project leader who fashioned his management style as an orchestra director to produce a harmonious result.

In Denver, Time Warner Cable's advanced engineering team converted an office into "the rubber room," where ideas were bounced off walls covered with whiteboards and block diagrams. Mike Hayashi brought a sharp wit and a sharp tongue for the technology suppliers that he would oversee. Louis Williamson grew up tinkering with washing machines and dreaming of being an oceanographer like Jacques Cousteau. Michael Adams previously worked in telecommunications in Ottawa, Canada. Ralph Brown earned a master's degree in speech recognition from MIT. Other Time Warner staffers were tapped for key management and development roles in New York, Stamford, and Los Angeles.

Now Ludington kept his tie on, staying in compliance with the company dress code. He needed to command a measure of respect before the wide assortment of new personnel, mostly in their twenties or early thirties. "We were so young then," he mused later.

Once they arrived in Orlando, the FSN developers set off on their mission, working twelve-, fifteen- or eighteen-hour days until some basically lived in the NOC. When they weren't on site, they were hopping planes to work with partners in Atlanta, Denver, Los Angeles,

New York, and Silicon Valley. Long nights of work slipped into beer and pool in a smoky bar best known as the Copper Rocket Pub but early on called the Road Kill Café. It was an ominous metaphor for people working on the Information Superhighway.

The developers were different than the engineer-nerd stereotype back then. These were not pale geeks wearing thick eyeglasses and pocket protectors. Some recruits carried New Age titles that were previously foreign to traditional television. Daniel Levy was "director of consumer interface." Hal Wolf, who came from HSN to manage the content applications business, was named vice president of programming. His title was changed to VP of content because the Silicon Valley coders thought his original title meant that he, too, was a computer programmer.

Many of the Silicon Valley coders worked for partner company Silicon Graphics, Inc. (SGI), selected by Time Warner to provide servers, an operating system (OS), in-home terminals, and other support. SGI was famous for building 3D graphics computer workstations used by Industrial Light & Magic, the visual effects studio founded by filmmaker George Lucas. SGI technology helped create what was said to be the first digital character in movie history, a shimmering, snakelike "pseudopod" in the 1989 film *The Abyss*. Among other films, SGI helped to bring dinosaurs to life in the 1993 hit *Jurassic Park*.

The Silicon Valley coders were well versed in the art of software, a skill set that was largely a mystery to cable and telecom engineers. But they were an unsettling presence, FSN workers recalled. They worked odd hours, flaunted the company dress code by wearing shorts and sandals, and downed caffeine until computer code practically shook out of their heads.

Ludington's NOC eventually filled up as the digital equipment arrived. The process had ignited many more arguments and much difficulty. Finally, his former handball court was transformed by large, hot, humming metal boxes glistening under fluorescent lights. The hardware was linked by interminable, twisted spaghetti strands of electric cords and connecting cables that snaked beneath a raised tile floor and filled cabinets. The NOC was bursting at the seams; Ludington had walls torn down to create space for a companion NOC to house a billing system and equipment for a potential telephone service.

Standing at attention were light-blue Challenge video server cabinets from SGI, each one initially costing about $1 million, according to Levin. The individual eight servers were as large as refrigerators and stood in neat rows, ready to be filled with digitized movies for on-demand consumption. As a cousin of Warner Bros., FSN named the servers after characters in the studio's Batman movie franchise: Batman, Robin, Joker, Penguin, Catwoman, Riddler, Mister Freeze, and Two Face. Racks upon racks of signal modulators and other gear were blasted by air-conditioning to prevent any meltdowns.

Inside FSN homes, the key component was the Home Communications Terminal (HCT) from Scientific-Atlanta (S-A) that would connect to TV sets and present interactive apps on consumers' screens. The boxes, looking like overstuffed VCRs, were a Frankenstein mashup of a powerful SGI computer and an advanced S-A cable set-top box. To combine the two devices into one was like trying to attach a rocket to a horse. Even in volume, the boxes cost about $4,500 each, Time Warner later acknowledged. No matter how you sliced it, the boxes cost more than fifteen times what a typical cable set-top box cost then.

Basic computing capabilities, such as memory storage and processing power, were absurd by today's norms. "It was wild," Ludington said. "Three-gigabyte hard drives were all the rage, and we're rocking out with huge cabinets of three-gig drives. Half a terabyte of storage took up half a room back then."

Today, anybody can buy a smartphone or other device small enough to fit in their pocket and carry dozens of times more memory storage. Modern-day cable engineers talk about storage in terms of petabytes—one petabyte equals one million gigabytes, enough to store more than thirteen years' worth of high-definition video.

CHAPTER 4
UNDER SIEGE

The FSN video servers were the size of refrigerators and had little storage capacity (photo courtesy of Tammy Snook Quezada, former VP, FSN communications).

A S A SCHOOLGIRL GROWING UP in Germany, where her military family was stationed, Yvette Kanouff first felt the spark that would lead her to a career in technology. One day in the eighth grade, her math teacher challenged her to solve an algebra problem on the chalkboard in front of the class. Kanouff went to the board and looked over the equation. Something clicked inside her, and suddenly, she knew what all those numbers meant. "I solved the problem, and I thought, *That was so easy*. And I fell in love with math that day," she said.

She attended the University of Central Florida for an undergraduate degree in pure mathematics and a graduate degree in applied mathematics. In addition to her math skills, she developed a strong will and confidence that are crucial to technology projects: fast learning, problem-solving, new approaches, calculating, and recalculating.

But before she applied those skills to FSN, she worked for defense contractor Lockheed Martin on the radar system for Apache helicopters. "It ties very much into what cable ended up having to do in the digital transition—figuring out how to do analog to digital, to do encoding and different encoding algorithms, to do transport and optics," she said in an interview for The Cable Center, conducted by Leslie Ellis, a longtime colleague of mine and a popular tech writer.

A friend at TWC, Johnny Greene, told Kanouff about the company's effort to convert RF (radio frequency) analog signals into digital and push them through fiber-optic cable. It sounded fascinating, and she inquired about an opening. Ludington hired her.

"I came to FSN because it was considered to be the 'bleeding edge' in technology in combining computer technology, image processing, and television," she said.

In addition to being a bright engineer, Kanouff was one of far too few women in tech circles, particularly in the cable industry. For many years at cable's annual SCTE Cable-Tec Expo conventions for tech suppliers and engineers, seeing a woman in attendance was like spotting a unicorn. Similarly, engineer Louis Williamson was one of too few Blacks in the industry. The cable industry used internship programs and nonprofit foundations to diversify its workforce, including The Walter Kaitz Foundation, which held an annual gala dinner in New York, attended by media luminaries to support inclusion.

Everyone recognized that digital technology held tremendous promise, but on the chart of human evolution, digital developers in the early 1990s had just emerged from the primordial ooze and were struggling to stand upright. "There were very few of us at the time," Kanouff said about the FSN software engineers. "Of the handful of us that were there, we all did our own work as opposed to teams doing it. We'd test all the software, make sure it ran, and test it more."

Writing the software to operate an untried digital network was tricky business. There were no off-the-shelf packages of ready-made software and few standardized protocols or codecs. There were few developer communities or help desks to rely upon. Key building blocks for interactive applications, including Java and HTML, didn't take hold until after FSN began. Many of the developers had been schooled on software, such as C++ and PostScript, which came out in the early 1980s.

"We had to build every spec from scratch—how to encode, create metadata, store, stream, deliver, modulate, transport, build applications, and more," Kanouff said. Writing long strings of code raised the danger that a bug or typo in one string would get passed along and create "commented code"—dead code. When things didn't work, it was a painstaking task to retrace steps, find the errant code, and correct it.

"We'd never really attempted to be involved in a software development effort like this," said Glenn Britt, then president of Time Warner Cable Ventures and later chairman and CEO of the cable company. "We found that virtually every big software project is late. The creation of software is really an amazingly archaic process. It's all very manual. It is inherently buggy, because the machine is kind of irrefutably logical—and we're not."

ONE OF THE MOST CHALLENGING tasks was the brute force integration that Ludington foresaw. Somehow, some way, the SGI operating system, the developer's user interfaces, S-A's set-top box functions, and newly digitized content—movies, video games, and shopping catalogs—had to all be combined and taught to play nicely together. It was one thing to prove that applications would work in SGI's test lab in Silicon Valley, but Kanouff had to make sure they would work live on the cable system in Orlando.

Meanwhile, the TWC management in Stamford was thrust into an unfamiliar role. Carl Rossetti, a TWC senior VP of corporate development who was adept at tackling new ventures, said, "We, Time Warner Cable, ended up acting as the systems integrator for this thing, which was surely not a skill set that we possess but one that we had to exercise."

From an apps perspective, perhaps the tallest order was to invent video-on-demand using full-motion video streaming. Not pay-per-view, not near-video-on-demand, but honest-to-God full-motion VOD. Streaming represented an entirely different way of distributing video than what the television industry was accustomed to.

With over-the-air broadcast TV, signals are widely dispersed by an antenna tower where any receiving antenna within range can capture it. Similarly with cable, encrypted TV signals are broadly dispersed through wires and then decoded by set-top boxes in the home. With on-demand content, an individual stream has to be delivered to each and every recipient's individual device. It's what, in technical terms, is known as multicast delivery (one to many) versus unicast delivery (one to one), the latter of which is what the internet is all about.

That means the developers would have to create a way for an individual household to order a movie, receive it, be able to use all the VCR-like trick-play functions, and then end the session. The FSN developers would have to reinvent virtually every part of television distribution.

But first things first. In order to stream movies, the developers needed movies in a usable digital format. Digitization would provide the means to turn the movie into a single stream of bits that could be delivered to an individual box connected to a TV so that it could be ordered on-demand and manipulated by the viewer.

Starting in the late 1980s, some producers and broadcasters started converting movies to digital for broadcasting using D-1 and

D-2 digital video standards and equipment initially introduced by Sony and Bosch-BTS. According to Chris Cookson, former head of Warner Bros. technical operations, there were numerous engineering challenges, including converting films, which run at twenty-four frames per second, to NTSC broadcast standards that use thirty frames per second.

To get movies, Time Warner sent senior VP John Newton to Hollywood to talk to the studios. Newton was an amiable exec who could pull together content partnerships and get everyone working for the common good. As senior VP of film programming for HBO in the 1980s, Newton led a negotiating team that licensed some $2-billion worth of feature film exhibition rights, according to his bio. Surely, he could get the Hollywood powers-that-be excited about the future of on-demand video. Newton began a tour of the major studios to get agreements to use their movies for VOD.

Newton got the door slammed in his face. "They did not go for it, even a little," he said.

Hollywood studios weren't keen to promote on-demand movie services if it might threaten their $12 billion in annual home-video revenue. Plus, the VOD concept was clouded by murky copyright issues and concerns about securing movies from piracy. Those fears weren't unfounded; pirates were sneaking camcorders into theaters to record movies and peddling bootleg tapes on city streets. If a VOD movie wasn't sufficiently encrypted or it ran "in the clear," meaning there was no protection at all, pirates would have a new treasure chest to plunder.

Home video retailers, banded in what was then the Video Software Dealers Association (VSDA), raised red flags about VOD and continued an effort to delay the release windows for pay-per-view movies. Studios typically released their new titles in home video well before they allowed cable operators to offer them in PPV. If the VSDA had its way, movies wouldn't be shown on PPV or VOD on cable until after they appeared in theaters, home video, airplanes, and hotels, maybe even outhouses.

Newton eventually appealed directly to Collins and Levin to pressure Warner Bros. to wrest away films from the sister studio so the FSN team could test them. They received one movie: *Under Siege*, a 1992 film starring Steven Seagal as a heroic loner who takes on a group of nuclear terrorists.

"We had *Under Siege* forever. It was the movie that we played over and over," Kanouff said. On a wall, someone put up a promotional poster for *Under Siege*, an apt description of the FSN work environment. "Those of us who were there from the beginning always laughed at that."

Increasingly, Hollywood became enamored with digital technologies. More filmmakers were using digital special effects, often fueled by SGI. The digital effects were typically composited into live action footage. The full movies were still delivered on film in big reels to movie theaters; the advent of digital cinema was years away. Digitizing films was underway but not a common practice. FSN began a couple of years before the introduction of commonly used scanners that converted each frame of an analog film into a digital format, as well as encoders for MPEG-2 digital compression, based upon Wikipedia histories.

Similarly, the practice of digital asset management, which later became commonplace in handling digital resources, was still emerging. The FSN developers had to figure out how to organize the video and audio files as well as the metadata—a movie's title, credits, synopsis, and technical information.

Near the NOC, FSN established its own Digital Production Center (DPC) to produce promotional materials and other fare, using computer graphic animations and videos. According to Levy, who managed the facility, the DPC was one of the first places to have Avid Media Composer, a widely adopted video editing software. "We also had a digital audio recording studio for voiceovers, sound effects, and some original music," Levy said.

CHAPTER 5
THE $2-BILLION MAN

The big, heavy FSN Home Communications Terminals cost about $4,500 each (photo courtesy of Barco Library, Syndeo Institute at The Cable Center).

AT THE TIME OF **FSN,** John Callahan was something of a hybrid. He was a telecommunications engineer who could talk in technospeak, yet he could dumb down jargon into plain English. What's more, he possessed a dry sense of humor and impeccable timing, which at one time gave him the ambition to become a stand-up comic. Engineering paid steadier and was more suited to his fortuitous career path. After graduating with bachelor's and master's degrees in computer science, his work in telecommunications got him inside Bell Labs and AT&T's

NOC for telephone service, a NASA-like mission control room full of tracking screens, computer monitors, and dozens of employees.

Callahan's work shifted to US West. When the Baby Bell plunked down a $2.5-billion investment in Time Warner, largely to get involved in FSN, Callahan became a top draft choice to join the project. For that, Carl Rossetti dubbed Callahan "the $2-billion man."

Young and eager, Callahan headed to Orlando, where he was scheduled to meet Jim Ludington inside the FSN NOC. Having been inside AT&T's high-tech facility, Callahan arrived and was surprised by what he saw.

"So I'm used to seeing AT&T's huge room, it's like a planetarium with all these screens showing networks of the United States and all over the world, and there's about two hundred people and red lights flashing, all kinds of space-age stuff happening. And then I go to their NOC in Orlando, and there's Ludington in an empty room, playing handball. It's completely devoid of equipment," Callahan recalled. He couldn't believe how absurd the situation was.

"Keep in mind, we're supposed to be providing service in April of that year. So I go to Denver to meet with the engineering team, and I'm thinking, *This is a cluster fuck. The emperor has no clothes.* And I'm going to be a project manager working on software, but I wasn't supposed to talk to SGI, even though they had the primary role in software."

Despite that apparent restriction, Callahan was sent to SGI "to see what's what." Based in Mountain View, CA, SGI was one of the hottest computer and software companies in Silicon Valley. Founded by Jim Clark, one of the leading pioneers behind computers and the web, SGI possessed the ability to provide FSN with key hardware, an operating system, and multimedia graphics, as well as an army of coders. SGI personified the ultracool digerati vibe that was running through Silicon Valley. That culture was changing the way businesses operated, how offices looked, and how ideas turned into products. In the parlance of the SGI coders, Callahan said everything was "way cool."

"When I went into Silicon Graphics, I saw guys on mountain

bikes on the third floor and people juggling and making espressos. They had these wild purple walls and an industrial design art deco motif. Guys with long hair and clothes that hadn't been washed in a couple weeks. All that stuff was like being back in school again." *Ahh*, Callahan thought, *way cool.*

As Callahan saw, SGI was like a Superman bizarro world that was the opposite of Time Warner or other cable and telecom concerns. While the normal course of action in a project like FSN would be to impose discipline and order into the developmental process, SGI seemed to eschew any type of discipline at all. Callahan and others noted that SGI developers rarely wrote out a developmental process and usually created products by the seat of their pants. Seemingly contrary to logic, this paradigm had led to SGI's success. They were especially proud of the role their equipment and software played in the creation of 3D dinosaurs for *Jurassic Park*.

That's not to say that SGI was made up of a bunch of grunge slackers who happened to be lucky at computer coding. According to Callahan and others, when it came to coding, they were extremely talented and worked their butts off. From the top execs on down, they were all in when it came to tackling a project and overcoming challenges. It was a free-flowing creative process. Their mantra, as they repeatedly told their Time Warner partners, was *software is an art*.

On the hardware side, SGI customized firmware to overcome heat and vibration issues that could affect how a hard drive played VOD movies, according to Callahan. Faced with similar issues, the computer industry developed thermally calibrated disk drives that alleviate overheating that can result from a spinning disk. Callahan believed SGI's optimization of drive performance was ultimately helpful in the development of DVD and DVR (digital video recorder) devices.

The SGI software engineers were passionate about changing the face of television, but some brought a decidedly computer-based orientation to the medium. That reflected a habitual problem whenever Silicon Valley developers attempted to impose their viewpoint on the

TV experience. To create FSN's first TV navigator, SGI employed a software engineer who didn't own a television set until SGI eventually bought him one. He created a mock 3D flight simulator in which viewers flew into a city and could order a movie by flying into a movie theater fronted by a giant hot dog.

"Everyone asked, 'What's with the hot dog?'" recalled Hayashi, who oversaw supplier relationships. "Apparently, not only didn't he watch TV, he'd never been to a movie theater either."

The hot dog navigator was replaced by a revolving user interface called the Carousel. SGI created it with input from TWIG—Time Warner Interactive Group, a new outfit in Burbank, CA, that Mike LaJoie headed. TWIG was to develop interactive apps. The Carousel featured a colorful, high-tech look unlike anything seen on TV before. Once on screen, it turned to offer images and channel numbers for movies, shopping, games, and other venues. In essence, it would serve as the carousel of color that was touted by Walt Disney's TV show.

Stories about SGI engineers became legend. Sue Whitehead, a project manager who joined Callahan as a loaned employee from US West, recalled an SGI software engineer who stayed up for days working on part of the project and then suddenly disappeared. When Time Warner engineers kept asking when he would return, SGI told them they didn't understand that software engineers need time to refresh themselves. After a week went by, Whitehead asked SGI, "At what point do you figure these guys don't come back?" The engineer never returned.

The SGI crew may have seemed like odd fish to the cable managers, but they brought a software orientation and a culture of innovation that was new to cable operations. SGI engineers came to realize important things about digital technologies. Two of SGI's top technology executives that worked on FSN, Jim Barton and Mike Ramsay, recognized how a hard drive could be used to store video and manipulate live TV streams. After FSN in 1997, the two cofounded TiVo, the first DVR, an invention that rocked the television world. Another SGI manager, Jeff

Barco, later became one of the heads of WebTV, an internet-over-TV service acquired by Microsoft in 1997.

Jim Clark sought to leverage the company's role in the cable industry, which then was akin to a closed-door club that wouldn't let in new players unless they knew the secret handshake. In an interview with *Cablevision* magazine, Clark urged cable operators to "get proactive" by embracing digital and multimedia. If cable doesn't do it, the telcos will, he said. Cable has an advantage that may "last five years, but surely not ten." He warned, "The question of cable's very existence is at issue."

Clark wasn't around at SGI to see FSN's fruition. Disagreements about the direction of SGI divided the company's leadership, in part over whether to continue to embrace interactive TV, according to various accounts. Clark, who departed and was replaced by Ed McCracken, moved on to focus on Netscape and then WebMD, which popularized online medical advice. Clark also gained notoriety by seeking to build the world's largest yacht, decked out with high-tech computer and automated sailing gadgetry. Clark's yachting adventure and Silicon Valley exploits were chronicled in Michael Lewis's book, *The New New Thing*.

While SGI seemed like the odd cousin from out West, Time Warner's other partner for Home Communications Terminals, Scientific-Atlanta, was part of the family. S-A president Sid Topol, a mensch to the cable industry, had guided TV's migration to satellite delivery. Topol shepherded HBO onto satellite for Levin in 1975, then Ted Turner with superstation TBS, Brian Lamb's C-SPAN, and Pat Robertson's Christian Broadcasting Network. New networks were bouncing off satellites, and S-A built the satellite dishes for cable operators to catch and distribute them. Orders for satellite dishes flooded in so fast that S-A couldn't keep up with the demand.

"It was a moneymaker for everyone from day one, including me," Topol told me during an interview to mark HBO's fortieth anniversary on satellite. "The satellite-cable connection is what made cable viable and what made billionaires today."

■ ▶ ▶▶

The neighborhoods for FSN were wired for fiber and coax in an HFC architecture. The network was built to 750 MHz of bandwidth. Ludington said it had a high-end return path, so it used 1 GHz total. It was plenty of bandwidth to carry the FSN applications and more than many cable systems that were built to 550 MHz.

To route on-demand video and interactive media, Time Warner purchased a gigantic ATM switch from AT&T Network Systems. ATM (asynchronous transfer mode; it has nothing to do with automated bank teller machines) was a key packet-switching technology for telecommunications. But it hadn't been used for routing video and audio before, and, as the engineers found out, it created unique issues.

Time Warner enlisted other major companies—including Andersen Consulting (which later became Accenture), Hitachi, and Toshiba—for various FSN development roles. Hewlett-Packard, the large supplier of copiers, faxes, and printers, took an interest in interactive TV and sought a role for its devices.

Toshiba, the large Japanese electronics company, was allowed to place one of its representatives in the NOC, under a confidentiality agreement. FSN staffers recalled that the Toshiba representative did not speak English, which added yet another odd element to the culture inside the NOC. At one point, the FSN managers came to suspect that Toshiba managers in Japan were communicating with their rep in Orlando about project information, a potential breach of the confidentiality agreement. Hayashi said he sent the Toshiba managers a warning in a language that anyone could understand. He placed his outstretched hand onto a copying machine, made a copy, and then faxed the picture of his hand to Toshiba management. It was a clear warning sign to stop what they were doing.

In May 1993, TWC named the Orlando neighborhoods for FSN, selected "because of their attractive demographic characteristics and educational system." The communities included a swath of Orlando's northern suburbs near Route I-4, including Wekiva, Lake Brantley, Sweetwater, and Spring Valley. The announcement was front-page news in the *Orlando Sentinel*, which said service would begin "in March."

Though April 1994 became officially regarded as the initial launch date for FSN, it's unclear when that date began to become publicly recognized. Whether it was March, April, or another month, the tight timetable, plus the public scrutiny, put heavy pressure on the developers. It was as if Orville and Wilbur Wright had a bunch of reporters hanging around their shop while they were piecing together their first airplane, saying, "You said this thing could fly—what's taking so long?"

CHAPTER 6
THE DIGERATI COMETH

As digital technology took hold, media companies engaged in a high-stakes battle for market dominance (*Cablevision*, photo by Craig Leddy).

A<small>S THE</small> **FSN** <small>DEVELOPERS WORKED,</small> America was getting involved in a budding romance with the home computer and about to get swept off its feet by the internet.

Time magazine named the personal computer its Machine of the Year in 1982. But it took time for techno-wary consumers to turn PCs into a mainstream purchase. By 1993, 22.8 percent of US households owned a PC, according to the US Census Bureau, and the number nearly doubled over the next five years. New models, marketed by

Gateway, Microsoft, Dell, and Apple, attempted to make it easier to use a PC than IBM devices that came with thick manuals. Although the PC was finally moving into the home, in 1993, about one-third of US households owned three or more TV sets, according to The Nielsen Company. In the living room, TV was still king, but the PC was muscling in.

And the internet? The adoption of the World Wide Web and introduction of browsers were making it a potential vehicle for media, telecommunications, and commerce. The web opened a floodgate of innovation, venture capital, and start-ups. Washington recognized that Silicon Valley was an engine to drive the US economy.

In 1991, Senator Al Gore, Jr., before excoriating the cable industry, promoted legislation, signed into law by President George H.W. Bush, which allocated $600 million for high-performance computing. That led to the creation of the National Information Infrastructure (NII). Gore referred to it as the Information Superhighway, a name that had a personal appeal for Gore since his father, former US Senator Al Gore Sr., championed the Federal Aid Highway Act of 1956 to support the creation of the interstate highway system. The NII initiative is credited with spurring internet development, including the Mosaic browser that was a key to web adoption.

Clinton's presidential campaign in 1992, now with vice presidential candidate Gore in tow, promoted the internet as a means to promote education, "the global village," and other common goods. Either by governmental fiat, piggybacking on the work of others, or pure luck, the internet made anyone associated with the NII look like a hero. (In 1999, Gore, then vice president, gave an interview with CNN in which he said, "During my service in the United States Congress, I took the initiative in creating the internet." He listed other initiatives that he had supported, but that statement led to public ridicule that he had claimed to have invented the internet.)

For new users, the problem with the internet was that it was constrained by the limitations of the access network and dial-up modems running through phone lines. Dial-up made horrendous sounds of static and high-pitched squealing before AOL users were greeted by a soothing voice saying, "You've got mail." Between the slow kilobit download speeds over twisted copper phone lines and business models based upon metered usage time, there was little hope for the concept of high-speed "always-on internet."

But the cavalry was on the way. The telcos worked on digital subscriber line (DSL) technology, and cable companies explored internet access through their fiber-coax architecture. Both had an eye toward a bigger internet concept: high-speed broadband. The betting line among financial analysts and industry pundits was that cable companies could not compete effectively and the winner in the race to provide broadband would be the telcos. Those predictions were dead wrong.

Meanwhile, the cooler people in the media industry, the digerati, espoused the coming glories of computer and media convergence. Others were fearful. Even before Napster decimated the music industry's business models, there were ominous feelings about what computers and the internet might mean for traditional television professionals and their careers. I recall going to industry conferences where broadcasting executives sought to tamp down enthusiasm for the internet. An ABC executive questioned whether the internet was like the CB radio fad of the 1970s. An NBC News executive said the notion that anyone would read news on a computer was ridiculous.

In a popular article in *The New Yorker* in February 1993, writer Ken Auletta described how Barry Diller, who had recently resigned as chairman of Fox, Inc. to become a partner in home shopping service QVC, was using a new Apple PowerBook laptop computer to run his life. "My odyssey began with the PowerBook," Diller said. It was like a religious awakening for him. And this was during a time when a laptop had limited capability and weighed about as much as a telephone book (kids, go ask your parents what a telephone book was). Auletta's article waxed poetic about Diller's sojourn:

Among other things, the machine helped Diller better understand the new video democracy. Through it, he could see how technology, with incredible speed, was transforming dumb television sets into smart ones, making it possible for viewers to select, organize, and interact with programming and information rather than passively consuming what was offered on fifty, or even five hundred, channels.

The PowerBook became for him a means of looking into the future, for he uses the laptop the way Apple Computer, which makes it, hopes that people will use a book-size machine, referred to as a personal digital assistant, that is right over the horizon. . . . Just as Diller could convert his laptop into a word processor, a fax, a file cabinet, a spreadsheet, a conveyor of commands, or a link to various networks of news or data, so in the next few years, he came to understand, viewers will receive video on demand—be able to watch what they want when they want. With the click of a remote control or a telephone button, they will summon up movies from the equivalent of a video jukebox. In an instant, they will send for and receive a paperless newspaper, a program they missed last night, a weather report.

Man, other media executives thought, *Barry Diller is so cool! Why aren't I that cool? I better get a laptop and figure this shit out.*

But, as hard as it might be to believe today, there remained plenty of skepticism in cable industry circles about the internet's future. During Western Cable Shows and other conferences in the mid-nineties, executives publicly debated whether the cable industry should take interest in the internet or not. Among those advocating that cable embrace the internet were Malone and Brian Roberts, the son of Comcast founder Ralph Roberts, who would go on to build Comcast into the biggest broadband provider in the US. I recall an audience demonstration by industry leader Steve Effros, who downloaded a photo of the White House onto a computer screen. As the photo slowly scanned onto the screen line by line, one couldn't help but wonder whether someday this would be a way to send video.

The companies that raced to embrace interactive TV were now looking over their shoulders at the internet, which was coming up fast. Plus, they were having trouble defining what interactive TV was. Did ITV mean interactive advertising and home shopping? Did it mean polling, playing along with game shows, or voting to change a show plot? Was ITV the same thing as what was known as teletext, in which you could get instant news, sports, stock quotes? Was VOD also ITV?

The differing viewpoints were based largely upon how various players sought to make money off the new medium. A new generation of developers was growing up in Silicon Valley, defining interactive TV as putting the internet on television. At industry conferences, panel speakers engaged in tiresome debates over the difference between a "lean-forward" experience like using a computer and a "lean-back" experience like watching TV. The industry's progress toward reshaping the TV medium was getting mired in posturing and semantics.

Robert Montgomery, who managed FSN applications business development, said, "Interactive TV was being defined on a daily basis."

THE BIGGEST CABLE AND MEDIA companies continued to seek their claim in the digital sweepstakes. In April 1993, TCI announced The Infostructure Network, a $1.9 billion, four-year fiber network upgrade to support its digital compression technology and offer more channels. TCI promoted the plan as a private-sector response to the federal government's call for an Information Superhighway—perhaps another way for Malone to tell the government to get the hell out of his way.

Cablevision magazine, while I was editor, featured a cover with a mock boxing poster, pitting Levin and Malone in a battle for the twenty-first century. The article chronicled the moves by the industry leaders, "one a Denver maverick, the other a New York sophisticate, in an ego-driven dual for TV's future. Who'll come out on top?"

In the article, Tom Elliot, TCI's head of cable technology, who grew up on a Montana ranch and typified the company's Western ethos, discussed the difference between TCI and Time Warner: "The difference is, Time Warner is fundamentally a programmer that happens to be in the cable business. We're the other way around."

Microsoft pursued relationships with both companies. In a retrospective for CableLabs, Malone recalled that Gates said he could "build a digital set-top box that would fully comply with the standards that we were looking for, in volume for under three hundred bucks." Reports surfaced that TCI and Time Warner were considering a joint venture called Cablesoft to develop standard ITV software. In 1994, TCI invested $125 million for a 20 percent share of Microsoft's MSN online service, *Cablevision* reported, although the publication noted that questions remained over whether Microsoft would become "a significant cable player or merely a luminous, distant orb."

Both the trade press and consumer press had a field day theorizing about what interactivity might bring. FSN was often portrayed as the place that would find the answers. An April 1993 *Time* magazine cover story on "The Info Highway" carried a section titled "When the Revolution Comes, What Will Happen to Channels? Networks? Commercials? Video Stores? Your Bill?" Based on what transpired over the ensuing years, those were all good questions.

Digital technology was spurring "Media Mania," as *BusinessWeek* trumpeted on its cover in July 1993. The cover showed photos of top executives' heads on top of animated bodies hovering in a dark, starry sky: Levin, Malone, Rupert Murdoch holding a television with the Fox logo, Sony's Mickey Schulhof sporting a Walkman, and Walt Disney CEO Michael Eisner with a movie camera. The article reflected the exuberance of the time:

What is digital technology, and why is it so tantalizing? Simply put, by converting words and pictures into digital form, programmers can send far more of them over wires and into TV sets. Suddenly, couch potatoes could receive 500 or even 50,000 channels. Digital technology also allows viewers to send messages back up the line. Where once you tuned in passively to *60 Minutes* or *Roseanne*, you'll now be able to interact with the tube. This opens the door to a dizzying array of TV services: home shopping and banking, long-distance learning, video games, even telephone service.

Not everyone believed in the vision, including Ted Turner. He was perennially vocal about cable, nuclear war, the environment, and his hatred for Rupert Murdoch. But when it came to interactive TV, he was relatively quiet. He told *BusinessWeek*, "The fact is, every interactive cable experiment so far has failed."

Turner had other distractions too. CNN continued to hemorrhage money, even though it had gained global respect for its 1991 coverage of the start of the Persian Gulf War, when correspondents Bernard Shaw, Peter Arnett, and John Holliman reported from inside the Rasheed Hotel as US bombs fell on Baghdad. The financial predicament threatened Turner's empire and eventually forced him into the arms of Levin.

If companies couldn't build their way into the digital future, they'd buy their way in. In May 1993, US West made its $2.5-billion investment in Time Warner, with $1 billion "earmarked for building cable Full Service Networks" and the remaining $1.5 billion going toward knocking down Time Warner's debt. Levin got a needed financial infusion, and analysts heralded the deal as a sign of the coming convergence between cable and phone companies.

■ ▶ ▶▶

While multiple cable, phone, and computer companies were making deals and jockeying for position, where was Steve Jobs and Apple? Apple was occasionally mentioned in reports and conversations about interactive TV, but nothing materialized. Partly, this may have been the result of Apple's need to concentrate on its own situation when it came to the brink of disaster after Jobs departed from the company, followed by his subsequent return and unparalleled success.

Despite sentiment that an alliance between Apple and cable would create a technological dynamo, Jobs is said to have wanted no part of it. Apple was part of the Silicon Valley digerati that turned its nose up at television. Many software engineers in the Valley didn't own a TV set, didn't care for its insipid content, and preferred to spend their spare time on their computers or playing *Dungeons & Dragons*.

Over time, various cable delegation trips and overtures were made to Jobs. Multiple sources reported a similar result. In one way or another, Jobs told them, "Why would I want to do business with the cable industry? I hate the cable industry."

CHAPTER 7
THE ORCHESTRA LEADER

Tom Feige and former president Bill Clinton, whose administration promoted the Information Superhighway (photo courtesy of Tom Feige).

BILL BROWN COULDN'T FATHOM WHAT was happening to his cable operation. He was president of Time Warner Cable's Central Florida Division, which included Orlando and other cable properties. With his white hair and white beard, Brown looked the old-school part, and he admitted it. Like most of his cable colleagues, he was not well-versed in digital's nuances. Yet he was a good Time Warner corporate citizen who ran a tight ship and produced positive financial results.

The corporate powers in New York and Stamford had foisted Ludington on him. FSN was an experimental project that, in his opinion, his local division should have controlled. That was bad enough. But now there were all these other people walking around in the building, including those software coders from Silicon Valley wearing shorts and sandals. Despite repeated requests, they didn't follow the business dress code like the Time Warner people were required to do. And everything they talked about was described as being way cool this and way cool that.

"This is a joke," Brown told Stamford corporate. "I won't be held responsible."

Brown told me the engineers "kept trying to make it better and better, not knowing when to stop." He liked to needle the engineers with a quip he learned from his days working in the aerospace industry: "There comes a time in every project when you shoot the engineers and start the project." His joke went over like a lead balloon.

Silicon Valley was the new cradle of civilization; everyone knew that. But did the managers from SGI have to flaunt it in everyone's faces? The cable people needed to learn that, as SGI managers told them, "Software is an art." Down in the trenches, the cable engineers and SGI software coders generally got along ("We were too busy trying to solve hard problems," Kanouff explained). But among the company managers, fundamental differences festered.

Glenn Britt, as a leader in Time Warner's business ventures, was accustomed to the culture clashes. "There's a big difference between traditional cable engineers who operate in an RF, analog world and digital engineers. There are different mathematical disciplines, and they just come from different worlds," he said. "Getting these two sets of people to work together and understand each other was a challenge. The digital guys tend to look down on the RF guys."

Chiddix characterized SGI management with three well-enunciated words: "Brilliant, arrogant jerks."

Tensions finally came to a head during a meeting in which SGI management sought to wrest control of the FSN project. According to those who were present, a top company official declared that SGI no longer wanted to work with any "cable Bozos," comparing cable managers to America's favorite TV clown.

Cable Bozos? Software is an art? How rude, how pretentious, how . . . maybe correct. When it came to computer software, "We *were* Bozos," Feige conceded. Cable was a hardware-driven construction business focused on set-top boxes, amplifiers, and coaxial cable. Interactivity required attention to operating systems, code, applications, and interfaces.

The SGI team really didn't want to be antagonistic. They confided in Callahan, seeking his advice to remedy the situation. Callahan advised them to give Time Warner more information about their progress. Perhaps, he offered, SGI could create a Gantt chart, which shows a timeline of a project and key elements along the way. Even though that may have seemed like a lot of planning by SGI's standards, the developers created the first project roadmap for the service and it was well received by everyone else, Callahan recalled.

Based on the ultimate fall of SGI from its industry-leading position (it filed for bankruptcy protection twice in the late 2000s), some of the cable engineers later wondered whether things would have turned out differently had Time Warner selected other potential partners that were in the running, including Microsoft and Sun Microsystems.

At the time of the tech selection process, Microsoft was adding multimedia capabilities to Windows, and Gates had signaled his interest in interactive TV. Sun was developing Java, a programming language introduced in 1995 that became widely used for internet applications. In the early 2000s, Java became a key part of the OpenCable Platform (OCAP), a middleware platform designed to facilitate interoperability between cable set-tops and digital TVs and provide a foundation for ITV apps.

For Callahan, SGI was the right partner. "They got it done," he said. "It didn't work one hundred percent in December 1994, but by about June 1995 the network was pretty stable for the next two-and-a-half years. The core of that system they built in less than two years. In software development, that's pretty remarkable."

■ ▶ ▶

RIFTS BETWEEN TIME WARNER AND SGI managers were just one place where cracks in the project foundation began to occur. Convergence may have been starting to occur between cable and computer technologies, but not necessarily the people behind them.

It didn't help that the organization behind FSN was, literally, all over the map: a corporation headquartered in New York; a cable division in Stamford; a project in Orlando layered onto a local cable operation; an engineering group in Denver; a content developer in Los Angeles; and tech suppliers in Silicon Valley, Atlanta, New Jersey, and Japan.

Time Warner brought in Andersen Consulting (now Accenture) to support development and bring organizational discipline to the project. But Andersen's presence also added to the complexity of personalities, languages, and cultures. Andersen produced a detailed roadmap of the FSN project, preferring to call the cable system CableWorks. Andersen's recommendations were often laden with techno-speak. An example: "Develop M&PM [marketing and performance measurement] Detail Filter interface to Message Processing System for scheduling and updating Message Processing Detail Filter rules." Later, Andersen's interactive activities were handled by its Infocosm Enterprise unit, "infocosm" being the company's own term for the convergence of computing, communications, and commerce.

The involved players didn't have a consistent view of what FSN even was. Some engineers believed they were working on a project that would change the world, while others regarded it as an R&D experiment. The public relations staff had to keep media interest high while attempting to manage expectations. In New York, Time Warner reps whipped up advertisers' enthusiasm for an interactive advertising platform that didn't exist.

Ludington tried to maintain his patience as he was subjected to the dress code, SGI's taunts, and the arguments between engineers. The project was careening out of control. He fired off a memo to Stamford.

"There is no driver on this bus!" he said. "Each group (Scientific Atlanta, SGI, Andersen) appointed program managers who are attempting to exert control, though a lack of fundamental direction pervades. Throw into the mix the separation of hardware and software subgroups, TWIG, another consultant or two, and all of the Time Warner players, and there is no explanation for what is underway."

The kumbaya feeling of leading the digital revolution was disintegrating into chaos.

IN STAMFORD, THE TWC BRASS felt Ludington's pain. The cable division was comprised of pragmatic managers who knew how to build cable systems, connect homes, forge contracts, sell services, collect bill payments, and make money. Fanciful projects were not TWC's style. It was important to keep up with the latest capabilities, but not if it meant putting the company's ample profits at risk.

When FSN was getting underway, the project was run by committee. Under Joe Collins, TWC created a leadership triumvirate consisting of Chiddix, Carl Rossetti, and Bill Brown. (After Brown's retirement in 1995, John Rigsby headed the Central Florida division.)

"FSN was a real management challenge. It was like herding cats," Rossetti said. "Everything we were doing was new, and there was no roadmap."

In Orlando, there were committees on top of committees. As Ludington pointed out, management by committee wasn't cutting it. TWC management needed a captain on-site in Orlando who could right this rudderless ship.

The company began a quick executive search for an FSN president. It reached into its own ranks to come up with Tom Feige, who'd started his cable career as a door-to-door salesman in Albany, NY. Tall and lanky, with a wave of dark blond hair, Feige was born in Chicago and raised in Cincinnati in a conservative household, his father an IBM sales manager. According to a profile piece published in the *Orlando Sentinel*, there was no alcohol permitted, Feige said, except for "the stuff my mom put on her hair." His viewpoint was idealistic. "I had all these wonderful ideas about changing the world." He was a fan of *Star Trek* and *Back to the Future*.

Feige had a flare for diplomacy and probably would have made for a successful politician. Thirty-nine at the time, he looked like a perennial college kid, though he could be the adult taskmaster when needed. With the odds stacking against FSN, Feige was like the rookie quarterback sent in to throw a Hail Mary pass that would win the game.

When Feige arrived at FSN, he initially relied upon his management skills developed as a supervisor of cable operations. "I was viewing a lot of my job as cost control, as trying to control everything just like I had done in the operating mode." That's a role, he notes, that includes giving staff specific tasks, setting boundaries, and establishing requirements that are fairly rigid.

"I did some research about what had occurred in successful development projects. I realized I was going to have to change my management style to one of allowing a lot more flexibility, less boundaries, and an agreement on goals that allows much more latitude from a creative perspective," he said.

"I knew we were going to have to make some mistakes and waste a little money if we really wanted to get these results in the timeframe, because we were going to have to try things that weren't proven and were untried. So I made a shift to kind of a less controlling, more developmental approach of managing creative people. I think it really improved the way our staff operated after that."

With the help of a management consultant and business

psychologist, Feige molded a management style to suit FSN's needs. He developed a metaphorical paradigm for his role: "You are the orchestra director, and it is your job to make sure that everybody has the resources, is well enough trained, and is well coordinated and motivated enough, with great understanding of what everybody else's part is so that they can effectively work together to bring a beautiful, harmonious result."

■ ▶ ▶▶

ANOTHER OUTSIDER WHO BROUGHT A new focus to managing the project was Sue Whitehead, who was involved in the growing 1990s fields of information technology (IT) and project management, a vital discipline for software-based endeavors. Working with AT&T and US West, she enjoyed studying how organizations work and bring technologies to life. As a loaner from US West, she brought her own microscope to independently examine the cell structure inside the FSN petri dish.

Whitehead arrived in time to witness FSN's transformation from a dysfunctional family to a productive operation. It took time to put together the key building blocks for successful project management: organization, leadership, goals, strategies, partnerships, communication, and skill sets. Due to the requirements for highly complex technology integration, the cross-cultural aspects of the organization, and the tight timeline, management decisions "always erred in favor of time," Whitehead found.

Feige was in charge in Orlando, and Rossetti was given more responsibility in Stamford. Rossetti recalled, "While Tom was trying to manage all the stuff in Orlando, I was trying to manage all the guys at Time Warner and not have them step all over each other."

Some executives wanted to get involved because they saw FSN as "a giant career booster," he said. "They thought this was going to be the greatest thing in the world, and if you were attached to it, your career would go up like a rocket ship. And some did. And unfortunately, some came back down, nose first."

FSN moved toward becoming a self-sufficient operation in Orlando. It was developing its own identity, structure, priorities, and staff. FSN became more task-oriented and moved away from using steering committees, except for weekly status calls. Task forces each had a narrow focus, with responsibility for specific results. Feige was creating a culture before the notion of culture became a widely recognized imperative in corporate America.

All of the participants needed to feel a high-level responsibility and a shared reward for an outcome that would provide a common good. Feige gathered input from the various cable and computer camps to create a mutually agreed upon FSN project mission statement: "We will lead the telecommunications revolution by merging cable, telephone, and computer technologies to enrich our customers' lives through greater choice, control and convenience."

It was a bold and ambitious rallying cry. In an analysis about FSN project management conducted with Andersen consultants, Whitehead maintained that the mission statement "created a sense of interdependence and shared destiny that encouraged individuals to look beyond their personal interests for the good of the program."

CHAPTER 8
HOME OF THE 21ST CENTURY

A 3,700-square-foot house was built to show off FSN services and electronic gadgetry (photo courtesy of Laura Nolte).

WHILE THE **FSN** PROJECT WAS racing to get up to speed, a young marketer named Bob Benya boarded a plane in Stockholm, Sweden, to make his way to Orlando. A graduate of New York University, Benya was working for a Time Warner international venture in Stockholm when the opportunity arose to head up marketing for FSN. Fresh into his thirties, Benya headed to Orlando for what seemed like a unique challenge, one that also could be a hell of a lot of fun.

Bob, or Bobby, as he was often called, had boyish clean-cut looks with blond hair. At some point in your life, you've probably known a Bobby Benya. Growing up, he was the kid with the perfect haircut, quick wit, and mischievous grin, the kind of guy who could do no wrong yet get away with murder. Odds are, Bobby Benya would be successful in any role that he took on, be it a marketing executive or soap-opera star.

Benya was to take on the marketing of FSN's services, a career path through unchartered territory, because none of the services existed before. No matter, he'd scope it out, apply himself, and make it his own. The parameters of the marketing task were unclear, so the sky was the limit. No idea was a bad idea. And it didn't seem like anyone was paying attention to budget caps.

But starting off, Benya found himself focusing on other things than marketing. He was scoping out real estate.

Benya got off the plane in Orlando, half asleep, and went directly to a meeting with Feige, newly installed as president of FSN. Feige told him that his first mission was to oversee the building of a new house—and the house wasn't for Benya.

"Feige said something about the house. I thought he was talking about *my* house, the house I was ultimately going to live in," Benya recalled. "The next thing I know, I'm at lunch with Burton Craige, who was the publisher of *Southern Living* magazine."

Craige told Benya that *Southern Living*, the venerable magazine of lifestyle and design, was keenly interested in the FSN project and had been talking with Time Warner management. Their idea was to build a house in Orlando that would showcase the latest home technologies, a home of the future, as it often was called. It would be officially branded as the Home of the 21st Century. *Southern Living* had experience in showcasing designers through its long-running Idea House program.

By building a house near the FSN NOC, the interactive service would be the centerpiece of home entertainment. Home electronics suppliers and designers, many of whom were *Southern Living* advertisers, would be given space to show off their latest wares. First,

Craige told Benya, they needed someone to help manage construction of the house, a modern 3,700-square-foot model with lots of open space for visitors and demo products.

"You don't typically see 'home construction' in the job description for VP of marketing," Benya said with a smile. But, being a good corporate soldier and energetic marketer, he dove into the project. With *Southern Living*'s help, architects, designers, and bankers were lined up. A plot of land in an upscale suburban neighborhood near the NOC was groomed for construction.

As head of FSN's marketing, Bob Benya was cast into unconventional roles (photo courtesy of Bob Benya).

The Home of the 21st Century made sense for Orlando, which, as everyone knows, is the epicenter of amusement parks and fanciful attractions. Orlando was the perfect place to show off the whizbang, futuristic wonders that Time Warner and other technologists would bring. Orlando already had its Hall of Presidents, and now it would get its Home of the 21st Century. They could even sell tickets to it.

The home would serve another important purpose. Time Warner could bring in consumers and let them play with the FSN services and other toys. It would provide instant consumer research, a "natural lab," as Benya called it, to get an inside glimpse of how consumers would react to new applications. Visitors to the home would become a built-in focus group providing valuable feedback. Based on that potential, dozens of manufacturers, designers, and marketers flocked to get their products into the home.

"Everybody just loved the idea," Benya said. "Next thing you know, we had about one hundred and fifty different suppliers signed up and agreeing to provide their goods and services in exchange for being promoted in the house." But things got sticky because the house couldn't open until FSN launched, and the launch was likely getting delayed. "So I had to hold all these people off."

The grand ambitions of the futuristic house didn't sit well with the neighbors. As construction commenced and the project gained notice in the local press, one of the neighbors at a nearby development invited Benya to meet at his house. Benya arrived for the meeting—and he was ambushed.

"When I got there, every single family in the community was at the house waiting for me. They wanted to know what our plans were and our intentions. They raised a lot of concerns about traffic, because we were getting a lot of press at the time. As a result of that meeting, the next day we installed electronic security gates at their development so that all of the different visitors to the home of the future wouldn't be driving through their development and running over their kids.

"So"—he sighed—"I got involved in gate installation as well."

THE FSN DEVELOPERS WERE GIVEN the opportunity to reinvent the TV medium, but that produced a lot of questions. What's the right content, design, and user experience? How do you present interactive services on screen and have viewers navigate through them? Would consumers interact with television? The developers were like an artist staring at a blank canvas and wondering where to begin.

"Not only had no one ever done this technically to make it work;

no one had ever really thought about how you present it to consumers," Feige said. "We spent huge numbers of hours brainstorming, talking to people, and getting input from as many different sources as we could to find a consistent consumer paradigm that we could rely on in terms of evolving television behavior from linear analog to nonlinear digital interactive."

The developers debated over the look and feel of graphical user interfaces (GUIs, pronounced *gooeys*), with their point of view often dictated by whether they came from a TV or PC background. They created a list of criteria that was four pages long and contained ninety-four questions, including "Where is it most appropriate to use sound in the user interface? What shortcuts would be most useful for experienced users? Should illuminated buttons be used? What percent of TVs are black-and-white? What special effects can or should be used to make the service more engaging or interesting without seemingly slowing down interaction or being distracting?"

The staff outlined a *Human Factors Workplan* to conduct twenty-two evaluations of questions related to on-screen interfaces. The evaluations assessed such matters as the usability of electronic program guides; the minimum type size for reading onscreen material from a distance of eight feet; how much punctuation is included in programming and movie titles; the development of a style guide for interactive applications; the minimum acceptable resolution for compressed video; and "how do book stores organize their content to facilitate shoppers?"

The developers were learning what type of interface design was attractive on TV and what was better suited for a PC. The SGI developers repeatedly told the FSN managers that the user interface has got to act "like a doorknob" that opens a door to interactive apps. Later, a former manager recalled, the SGI developers perplexed everyone by saying that the interface should be used like "a washing machine."

In many ways, these interface issues were the same as those confronted by early developers of websites. The concept of "search and discovery," which is highly important in finding video streaming programs today, had not surfaced yet. In the 1980s and early 1990s, viewers suffered through frustratingly slow program girds that scrolled to display a limited number of channels at a time. It's no wonder that consumers ended up "grazing" on channels, as the industry called it, because they really had no choice other than to flip through channels in hope of finding something they liked.

To find programming, most Americans relied upon TV listings in their local newspaper, various cable guide magazines, or the popular twice-weekly *TV Guide*. It had a circulation of 17 million when Rupert Murdoch purchased it in 1988 for $3 billion. In 1990, *TV Guide* added VCR Plus+ codes to program listings, a means for viewers to automatically record shows. The concept was invented by Gemstar International, which later purchased *TV Guide* and became a litigious protector of its patents on interactive guide technology.

FSN hosted a developers conference in early 1994 to speed development along. TWIG aided applications development by creating a cross-platform tool, which it called "arch angel," to bridge software differences. Daniel Levy developed a style guide to police applications development and coordinate technical guidelines for certification.

In New York, Thayer Bigelow, president and chief executive of Time Warner Cable Programming, had his staff explore interactive programming concepts for basic cable networks. As fate would have it, that would prove to be a fortuitous turn in Ludington's personal life.

The developers also had to rethink the TV remote. For VOD, the remote needed additional buttons for play/pause, rewind, and Fast Forward. It needed directional arrows—up, down, forward, and back—to navigate around interactive apps and play games. Working with the S-A manufacturers, the developers came up with a Select button to purchase items. At the bottom of the remote, they added buttons A (triangle), B (square), and C (circle) to handle various functions. These button formats became ubiquitous in TV remote design across the cable and satellite industries.

There was another important reason for creating a new remote.

A key factor in interactivity is to provide instantaneous information retrieval and avoid any lag time. Throughout the entire delivery chain, the turnaround time from a viewer's click of the remote to getting their requested content must be infinitesimal. "That's what made it so goddamn hard," Callahan said.

The response time for a remote click needed to be low, on the order of 100 milliseconds (ms). At the time, no wireless remote using infrared [IR] communications could go below 300 ms, according to Callahan. Installing a faster processor inside, the FSN remote handled the IR transfer in 50 ms. "That had never been done. Remotes of the day were much, much slower," he said.

Still, the engineers had to reduce every millisecond they could. The HTC had to process a request in less than 50 ms; then the server had roughly 20 to 30 ms to process the request, and it took about 50 ms to respond to the box and react to the user. "So a second or two from order to reaction," Callahan said.

Their efforts foreshadowed pursuits today to reduce the response time in streaming, gaming, robotics, and artificial intelligence to achieve what's known as low latency. In online video games, such as kill-or-be-killed Fortnite contests, low latency is crucial for instantaneous twitch responses. Betting on a sporting event is constrained by delays between the live action and the streamed broadcast, which can lag behind by thirty seconds or more. For self-driving cars to become a reality, there can be no lag in the transmissions that are piloting them. Today's broadband providers and 5G mobile services are striving for latency of less than 1 ms.

In focus groups for FSN, consumers debated over such things as the color and configuration of the buttons on the remote and how a set-top box should work. Feige recalled one focus group's suggestion that since Florida is a habitat for lots of insects, the set-top box should emit a tone to keep cockroaches and other bugs out of the house. The participating consumers were excited about being part of this futuristic experiment, although the researchers had to soothe some concerns that cable bills would soar and that interactivity might have a dehumanizing effect.

■ ▶ ▶▶

With the development of interactive content, FSN became the cult of innovation that Levin was striving for. FSN had no shortage of interested content providers who wanted to use the service as an interactive testing ground. Dozens of potential partners met with FSN or TWIG, including HBO, CNN, *Sports Illustrated*, the *Orlando Sentinel*, Pizza Hut, *Spiegel* catalogs, and the US Post Office.

But Levin also saw how difficult digital transformation would be, especially when facing self-imposed deadlines. Later, he said, "When you got into the digital domain, it was like 'Katy bar the door.' No one—no one—ever met any timetable. So it wasn't just the culture differences; it was that you really entered something that, in terms of production, distribution, and even the box in the home, had totally different characteristics from what we were used to working with."

The concept of interactive TV was inspiring others to think about TV from a creative standpoint and breathe new life into the medium. TV had long been ridiculed as a low-brow art form that may have been lowering America's collective IQ. In 1961, FCC Chairman Newton Minow declared TV to be a "vast wasteland." TV networks were accused of dumbing down TV by offering "lowest common denominator" shows to attract the most eyeballs. Elvis Presley famously shot his TV with a .44 Magnum.

With the potential addition of interactive elements to content, TV producers envisioned ways to personalize the viewing experience. Viewers could engage more deeply with programs and the actors. They could play along with game shows, express their opinion about characters, and answer trivia. What if viewers could alter the plot of a show or watch alternative endings? Interestingly, most of these concepts never went beyond the idea stage.

Madison Avenue also took keen interest in the Orlando plan. In the 1990s, TV commercials showed you the glories of Hot Pockets, Mentos, and breaking off a piece of that Kit Kat bar. But it was a one-way conversation. With interactive TV, consumers could potentially use their TV remote to get free samples, order a brochure on the latest car models, and make purchases, which then would be delivered by mail. Beyond catalog shopping (later known as t-commerce, a TV equivalent of e-commerce), interactive advertising could unleash the power of big brands on TV. Through the concept of addressable TV, targeted ads could be customized for individual homes based on their demographics, personal preferences, or buying habits.

In New York, Time Warner, largely through Geoff Holmes, began talking with major brands and ad agencies. Ford and Procter & Gamble were among the early interested advertisers. Press reports and industry analysts forecast billions of dollars in new revenue that could be generated through ITV advertising. But with all the other tasks that the FSN team had to perform, developing interactive ads for a small sample of homes slipped down the priority list.

For weeks, the FSN teams' brainstorming and creativity went on through long days that spilled into long nights at the Copper Rocket. By all accounts, the FSN staff embraced the 1990s ethos of "work hard, play hard." As Benya surmised, "Some of the best ideas were scribbled on the back of cocktail napkins."

WHILE CREATING THE APPLICATIONS WAS difficult, the devices to run them, the Home Communications Terminals, posed unique challenges. The HCT, a combination of SGI's Indy workstation and Scientific-Atlanta's 8600x advanced analog converter, got so hot that a special fan needed to be installed in the back. Developers had to find the perfect fan that would cool the unit but be quiet enough so that viewers could hear their movies and shows.

If the fan inside the HCT wasn't strong enough to cool the box, there was the haunting possibility that the HCT would overheat and burn down someone's house. The box was so heavy that it could crush people's TV stands or break through shelving.

So FSN offered customers a free furniture stand to support the HCT. The task of finding a sturdy console fell to Benya, another unique duty to add to his marketing role. He searched around Orlando retail stores to find the right model and made a large order.

"So now I was in the furniture business," Benya said. He burst out laughing. "You can't make this stuff up."

CHAPTER 9
NONE OF THE TOYS SMOKED

As CONTENT, TECHNOLOGIES, AND PARTNERSHIPS fell into place, the lineup of initial FSN applications took shape: navigation guide, movies on demand, catalog shopping, convenience shopping, games, and news and information.

Among the proposed apps (before anyone called them apps), the prospect of on-demand movies was the most intriguing. But the developers still had to figure out how to send a stream of a digitized movie, which they finally possessed, to a box where it could be received, displayed, and managed.

In Ludington's house near the NOC, he and Williamson transformed the dining room into a makeshift lab to test real-world delivery of a streamed movie from the cable headend.

"The dining room had no furniture anyway—what bachelor's house does?" Ludington said. "We set up folding tables on all three walls, and they were cluttered with computers, screens, keyboards, TVs, FSN boxes, S-A boxes, network test equipment, phones, flip charts, notebooks, etcetera." The kitchen was littered with coffee cups and stale pizza, but no food or drinks were allowed at the tables, to prevent a coffee spill or dollop of melted cheese from wrecking the multimillion dollar project. For much of the life of the lab, the dining room was a site of trial, error, and frustration.

After multiple attempts, the engineers couldn't figure out why a streamed movie wasn't showing up on their TV sets. Maybe it was sunspots, bad karma, or digital dystopia—who knew? But they pressed on. "It was just, 'Shit, we're making it work,'" Ludington said.

"Table, table, table against three walls with all sorts of stuff on them, and we're trying to figure out how and why we're not able to see anything," Ludington recalled. "And then—boom!—we're streaming to my house. Hey, it fucking worked! That was the breakthrough moment. That was where everyone is hooting and hollering and going to get hammered that night. Because after weeks and weeks of twelve-, fifteen-hour days, you actually got something from that headend to the lab that was set up in my dining room out in the neighborhood."

A bevy of Time Warner executives headed down to take a look. During an internal FSN demonstration at Ludington's house, in December 1993, a year before the public launch, Levin and other top executives, including Joe Collins, Jimmy Doolittle, Glenn Britt, and Carl Rossetti, watched as engineers streamed *The Fugitive*, a Warner Bros. thriller starring Harrison Ford. The digitized movie was routed from a server in the NOC through an ATM switch and delivered over coaxial cable to a TV. MPEG-2, the digital compression standard that became ubiquitous for cable digital video, was still emerging, so the engineers used "about MPEG one and a half," Ludington said. The executive team also reviewed early versions of the gaming and shopping apps.

"It was wild," Ludington said. "We had everyone down, crammed into my house." Outside, a thunderstorm rumbled through Orlando and produced a veil of rain and fog. Walking into Ludington's house, Levin slipped on the wet back-porch steps, and his legs went out from under him. Luckily, Ludington and Collins were behind to catch him, or he might have hit his head and perhaps not been a part of FSN's launch, let alone continue as the CEO of Time Warner. "It would have been a different thing," Ludington deadpanned.

"*The Fugitive* was the first digitized film that met FSN specs—special kudos to Warner Bros. for that feat," Benya said. "We didn't know if it would work. But after loading it onto the network and streaming it, there were lots of sighs of relief and smiles as we watched it, used trick play functionality, and accessed the metadata and box art."

The video streaming demo was a welcome sign. Assessments of the demo led to the oft-repeated engineering quip "None of the toys smoked." For those who saw streaming for the first time, that was a eureka moment. No matter what the potential result of the other interactive TV applications, everyone was fairly convinced that on-demand movies—true VOD—would be a game changer.

SPEED TO MARKET. **IT WAS** becoming a mantra in digital business. Those who were first to market with a new creation would leave all others in the dust. It's a maxim that did indeed produce some early winners, but it also resulted in untold numbers of product failures and company shutdowns. When speeding to market, beware of the speed bumps.

The Baby Bell telcos, not accustomed to fast-pace development, sought to muscle their way into the television distribution business by way of their ample checkbooks. They engaged in a wave of acquisitions and investments in cable, promoted under the banner of convergence. The starting point was with cable's biggest dealmaker, John Malone.

On a crisp day in October 1993, I was standing on a Metro-North train platform ready for my morning commute into Midtown Manhattan, where *Cablevision* magazine was headquartered. I unfurled my daily *New York Times* and stared at the headline. A friend was talking to me, but I couldn't seem to understand a word she was saying. "I'm sorry," I said as my mind swirled, "but the biggest deal in the history of our industry just went down."

"A Merger of Giants," the front-page headline blared. Bell Atlantic, a regional Bell operating company (RBOC), agreed to buy TCI for $33 billion. *What?* I thought. *Malone sold to a telco?*

"This is the perfect Information Age marriage," declared Ray Smith, chairman and chief executive of Bell Atlantic. I took a breath and recognized that, knowing how smart Malone was, it was clear he wasn't just taking a buyout so he could go off to sail on his boat in Maine. Malone would become vice chairman of Bell Atlantic, and, if the plan was fully executed, he stood to make $1 billion in stock options. Bob Magness, the TCI chairman, would make $1.5 billion. And was Ray Smith going to remain in charge? Doubtful.

The breakup of AT&T in 1984 created RBOCs, but they were constrained from getting into "electronic publishing," including the cable business, because each of the spinoff Baby Bells was large enough to swallow the entire cable industry whole. But the RBOCs were allowed to invest in out-of-territory cable systems. The Bell Atlantic acquisition was the biggest among other announced deals:

- Southwestern Bell announced an initial investment of $1.6 billion for 40 percent of a cable partnership with Cox Enterprises.

- In another deal, Southwestern Bell purchased cable systems headed by Gus Hauser in the Washington, DC, suburbs for $650 million.

- US West said it was paying a total of $1.2 billion to acquire Wometco Cable and Georgia Cable Television, two companies that served the majority of Atlanta.

- From the north came Bell Canada investing $275 million in Jones Intercable, founded by entrepreneur Glenn Jones.

- NYNEX Corp., the Bell spinoff serving much of the Northeast, invested $1.2 billion in Viacom.

Sumner Redstone, chairman and CEO of Viacom, used the NYNEX investment to outbid Barry Diller and purchase Paramount Communications in a $10-billion deal. The Paramount purchase helped Redstone amass networks, including CBS, MTV Networks, BET, and Showtime Networks, to support his creed that "content is king." (Redstone is credited with coining the phrase in 1994 while others credit Bill Gates, who wrote an essay with that title in 1996. It's also been traced back to authors in the 1970s.)

Other RBOCs planned their own ventures: BellSouth announced it would develop an interactive media trial with 12,000 homes in an Atlanta suburb. Ameritech, based in Chicago, planned to build its own digital video network in what was known as video dial tone (VDT), a service that could potentially skirt the AT&T consent decree restrictions on entering the cable business.

To carry data over copper phone lines, telcos planned to use asymmetric digital subscriber line (ADSL) technology, too slow for video. To boost their prospects, telcos tested fiber, microwave, and other technologies to provide more capacity for VOD and interactive services.

Mixing cable and telephone company cultures was like oil and water. The cable guys may have seemed old-fashioned by Silicon Valley standards, but they possessed an innovative spirit that made the telcos look ancient. The phone executives grew up in an era when AT&T was a common carrier intent on producing reliable stock dividends. Many observers wondered how the phone and cable guys were going to get along. The answer: they didn't.

Neither the Bell Atlantic-TCI merger nor Southwestern Bell-Cox partnership lasted more than four months. In press reports about the collapse of their mergers, parties blamed the FCC for regulating cable rates and undercutting the value of their deals. But regulators and some analysts doubted that was the real reason.

The US West-Time Warner relationship also turned frosty. In 1995, US West sued Time Warner to block its bid to buy TBS, and the telco sought to take greater control of the TWC cable systems. The TBS deal went through anyway.

The concept of convergence drew ridicule. As publisher Bill McGorry, my boss at *Cablevision*, joked, "Convergence is the future—and always will be."

■ ▶ ▶▶

IN ORLANDO, VOD HAD ITS breakthrough moment, but other FSN applications were posing enormous challenges. The mandate for catalog shopping in those pre-Amazon days posed many questions. The biggest challenge was enabling access to vast product lines and fulfilling purchases, especially while working with limited memory storage.

The developers created a virtual shopping mall using high-tech 3D city flyover graphics from SGI. Users could press the arrows on their remote to enter the mall and go into stores, including Crate & Barrel, Spiegel, Best Buy, Sharper Image, and Warner Bros. The service enabled users to change the color of sample window treatments, sweaters, and bathing suits. Users could make credit card purchases and then receive an order confirmation printout from a Hewlett-Packard printer that was connected to the HCT.

From the same dining room where VOD was hatched, Ludington made the first interactive shopping purchase. If you search the history of interactive shopping and e-commerce, you'll find a lot of claims about the first online purchase. It was new, exciting territory for many innovators and entrepreneurs. Home shopping had already proven its viability as consumers used their phones to buy products through cable's HSN, launched in 1985, and QVC, which launched the following year. After Tim Berners-Lee debuted the World Wide Web in 1991 and it opened to the public in 1993, purchases were made that foreshadowed online marketplaces like Amazon and eBay.

Add to those events a purchase made by Ludington through the Warner Bros. virtual store. "We ordered it from those tables in my house, and it showed up some days later. A Bugs Bunny Carman Miranda Cookie Jar—of all things!" It was a porcelain cookie jar in the shape of Bugs Bunny, dressed like Brazilian performer Carmen Miranda with a fruit hat, lipstick, and rouge.

The first item bought through FSN interactive shopping: Jim Ludington's Bugs Bunny Carman Miranda Cookie Jar (photo by Jim Ludington; product by Warner Bros., Looney Tunes).

The FSN virtual mall had a cutting edge look, but moving through it virtually proved to be slow. The number of products per brand had to be limited. Less complicated were the convenience shopping apps—the ability to order pizza from Pizza Hut or stamps from the US Postal Service, delivered by a mailman the next day.

For an interactive news service, FSN joined with the *Orlando Sentinel* to develop The News Exchange (TNX), which provided on-demand access to headlines, sports, weather, and business, plus time-shifted ABC and NBC news programming. Among those involved in the TNX development project were Walter Isaacson, who went on to head CNN and became a famous author of biographies, and Paul Sagan, who helped to develop the NY1 news channel in Manhattan. John Haile, editor and VP of the *Orlando Sentinel*, then owned by Tribune Co., credited TNX for completely changing the way the newspaper thought about news delivery—from acting as a once-a-day newspaper distributor to being a round-the-clock digital outlet.

FSN had to blend digital and analog assets to create a consumer service. The VOD and ITV applications were in the digital realm, while the linear TV channels were still analog. The Carousel navigator served as the gateway to the interactive venues and the on-demand home video theater. For regular TV, Prevue Guide, founded by United Video Satellite Group, provided a more traditional grid guide of TV channels. A big difference was that the Prevue Guide was interactive, enabling viewers to use their remotes to flip through channels on the grid, a vast improvement over electronic program guides that automatically scrolled through channel lineups at a maddeningly slow pace.

Hardware and software development moved in a chicken-and-egg dance, where the apps couldn't run without completion of the OS, and the OS itself depended on the hardware. Ultimately, the cable engineers had to decide which apps were capable of running on the new digital network. The apps developers in Orlando facetiously referred to the Denver advanced cable engineers as "The Seagulls," because, as they put it, the engineers would fly in and crap all over everything.

LaJoie, head of TWIG, noted that some engineers were working on hardware, others were creating software to run the network, while still others were writing applications. And somehow all their output had to be integrated into a seamless service.

"It was like trying to develop seats for a car without having a car to put them in," Lajoie said. "It was very fluid."

Software engineers worked at a frantic pace and left files full of commented code. The planned launch date of April 1994 was rushing toward them. The developers needed more time, time, time: time for stress tests to determine peak performance limits; "soak time" to debug software systems; and time to upgrade subscriber management and billing systems so customers could pay for these new digital wonders.

Feige summed it up: "All of these different software engineers are writing all of this code, and it all had to be integrated together so it worked, and it was all written differently. And so the process of getting this to work and to debug it was a huge, complicated process. It involved getting engineers to work with other engineers to work with other folks to make sure that each hook and each element interfaced appropriately with a myriad of elements at exactly the right time, in the right place, without error."

It became abundantly clear: A launch in April 1994 was impossible.

TIME WARNER RECOGNIZED THAT THE company needed to postpone the launch and address it publicly. "We decided it would be better to take control of that issue rather than let it dribble out, and then it would seem like you were covering it up," said Mike Luftman, VP of communications for TWC.

Luftman, who worked with TWC communications chief Lynn Yaeger in Stamford, became a primary spokesperson for the project, along with Tammy Lindsay in Orlando. Luftman was a straight shooter, not prone to hyperbole. He typically told reporters what was going on and let the chips fall where they may. Because with a new, untried project, who knew where the chips might fall.

SGI and S-A, who had been pointing fingers at each other for component delays and other matters, expressed concern over who would take the blame publicly. Luftman said, "I had some very difficult discussions with the respective heads of PR at those companies, who were blaming each other, and I guess us too, because they kept saying you guys changed the specifications, so it's your fault. It was fairly contentious."

On March 1, 1994, TWC issued a press release saying that FSN would roll out in the fourth quarter. It said the new timeframe will "allow additional refinements of the underlying system software and the set-top terminal." It included statements from TWC, SGI, and S-A executives affirming their commitment to the project. The release said, "Plans remain in place to have 4,000 customers on the network by year-end," although that number of homes was looking highly unlikely.

News outlets pounced on the company. Reuters said, "In what could be a significant setback for the development of a nationwide interactive television system, Time Warner Cable said Tuesday it will delay offering its interactive network to customers in Orlando, Florida, until the fourth quarter." A *Variety* headline trumpeted, "TW Finds Roadblock on Infopike." *The Hollywood Reporter*, citing issues with TCI's compression plan and other industry setbacks, said the delay "was the latest in a flood of bad news for the cable industry that has many beginning to wonder if the information highway is destined to become an unused two-lane blacktop."

BusinessWeek, which a year before had been touting Media Mania, ran a 1,200-word piece under the banner, "Interactive TV: Not Ready For Prime Time," and said "the Information Superhighway remains shut down as construction work continues." Industry analysts piled on, with a Yankee Group analyst telling the *Orlando Sentinel*, "The only way in which it could be viewed as a surprise is the assuredness that Time Warner has been putting forth that it would begin in April."

Despite the negative tenor of the stories, Feige said the reaction wasn't all that surprising to the FSN staff. "I think we expected a bigger reaction than we got when we ultimately made the announcement," he said. "No one in the group felt that they could have done anything more to have gotten us where we needed to be."

Chiddix told *Multichannel News*, "It bemuses me to no end that [the delay] was treated as though the whole project had crashed and was a failure. You would think that the business press would have realized that this isn't the first time a highly complex software project has been delayed."

About the same time that the FSN delay was disclosed, Bell Atlantic announced plans to build a 172,000-square-foot digital production center in Reston, VA, to convert films and videos into

MPEG digital and launch its VOD-rich Stargazer service. The telco said it licensed software from Oracle, headed by Larry Ellison, another mogul moving into the ITV game.

■ ▶ ▶▶

ALTHOUGH BARELY ANYONE NOTICED, MANY of the FSN services promised during the January 1993 press event were scuttled. An early casualty was telephone service. According to the managers, the leading technological contender was an emerging mobile-like phone capability, personal communications service (PCS). But including it would raise the technological hurdles even higher. Time Warner also faced the possibility of protracted regulatory proceedings at the Florida Public Service Commission to become a carrier. Such oversight possibly could have exposed interactive services to regulations as well.

Meanwhile, the company began to back off the promise of serving 4,000 homes at the start. At a conference in September 1994, Mario Vecchi, VP of network engineering for TWC, said the incredible complexity and the need for an operational support system capable of handling real-time transactions would reduce the number of previously scheduled subscribers. *Broadcasting & Cable* quoted Tammy Lindsay saying, "It is not possible to say exactly how many customers will be hooked up when we launch in the fourth quarter."

Mario Vecchi was among a growing legion of executives whose attention was gravitating toward the internet. He developed a presentation for TWC titled "PC-based Services: Home and Business-to-Home Datacom." The presentation discussed the internet, cable modem developments, and how "our cable plant gives us a unique advantage in reaching the homes with high-speed datacom services." Vecchi would go on to head Road Runner, TWC's internet service, and then America Online, the one-time partner of Time Warner.

For some time, interest in the internet had been brewing in various parts of the company. At Time Inc., Walter Isaacson, then an editor at *Time* magazine, had gotten an early glimpse of the internet's potential on New Year's Eve 1992, according to *Riptide*, an online history project devoted to "the epic collision between journalism and digital technology." At the urging of a writer, he borrowed a dial-up modem and went on to the Well, an early online bulletin board, and thought, *Whoa, there's this whole cyber community*. Soon, the company was talking about putting its magazine content online through emerging services AOL, CompuServe, and Prodigy Communications Corporation, then putting its magazines directly online.

Levin, in a *Riptide* interview, recalled that Isaacson later "came into my office and said, 'There's something called the World Wide Web. You ought to take a look at it.' It showed that somebody had finally figured out a unification strategy," Levin said. "Somebody brought an agreed-upon standard so that all parties could have access to signing on and getting something back. That there was a universal code. I thought that was transformative."

In January 1994, Isaacson sent a memo to Levin saying that after his visits to FSN and the MIT Media Lab, which was championing digital innovations under Nicholas Negroponte, "it has become clear to me that we are about to see a radical change in the way that news is delivered." He proposed using FSN as a launching pad for a news and information service distributed to PCs.

"Such an information service could make use of the broadband capacity of cable to deliver pictures and some video as well as text. Users would be charged an hourly connect charge for the service, plus extra fees for access to other commercial services," Isaacson wrote. The service would leverage Time Inc. content as well as materials in the public domain. Plus, it could serve as a gateway to Prodigy, AOL, CompuServe, and Delphi, which were paying for phone-line access and that "we could collect instead," he said.

By the end of that year, about the same time as FSN was scheduled to launch, Isaacson's plan had evolved into a broad new media strategy and an online service called Pathfinder. Though the initial online service was primitive, Pathfinder webmasters planned to expand it throughout 1995 by adding functions for user registrations and passwords, advertising, credit card transactions for shopping services, and a portal to wide range of content from Time Inc. and outside sources.

Isaacson told me Time Warner's interest in online activity "grew right out of FSN." Isaacson went on to become *Time*'s top editor in 1996 and chairman and CEO of CNN from 2001 to 2003. He's probably best known as the author of popular biographies on Albert Einstein, Benjamin Franklin, Henry Kissinger, Steve Jobs, Leonardo da Vinci, and Elon Musk.

CHAPTER 10
LAUNCH DAY AND THE OH JESUS SWITCH

Jerry Levin on stage prior to the FSN launch (photo courtesy of Laura Nolte).

IN FALL 1994, LEVIN AND other top executives were back in Orlando. It was go/no-go decision time for an FSN launch. Benya recalled that it was a Sunday afternoon and Levin was playing with an FSN remote at Ludington's house. After a while, Levin asked, "So, are we going to do this?"

Chiddix was present and assured Levin that the launch could be pulled off. The network's stability was shaky, and the primary applications were still being completed, but they could be shaped up for a live demo to a limited number of locations. Following the April 1994 postponement, Time Warner had promised a launch in the fourth quarter. Everyone was growing tired of the constant references in the press to the "much-delayed FSN." A grand event was in order, one that would show off FSN's accomplishments and Time Warner's digital leadership.

Levin went around the room and had everyone give their answer. With varying degrees of enthusiasm and caution, everyone agreed: Let's do it.

But when? The executives pulled out their day planners to review dates (most used some form of paper planning calendar before Blackberrys became a ubiquitous tool at Time Warner). The team wanted as much preparation time as possible without having the launch event bump up against the holidays. After a lot of schedule comparisons, they came up with a date: December 14.

Levin turned to Benya and said, "The house needs to be ready, because we're coming to the house," referring to the Home of the 21st Century. Levin's brown eyes bore into Benya's blues. "So, will you be ready?"

Benya's mind instantly flashed across the home itself and the excess of unfinished tasks: the open walls awaiting wiring, the attic being stuffed with servers, rooms requiring fresh paint and furniture, and empty walls that needed art, maybe even a few house plants tossed around. They had to rally all of the *Southern Living* vendors so they could install their gadgets and make sure they had adequate wiring and electric power. They needed to be certain that the air-conditioning would hold up while on full throttle. Some local residents needed to be enticed into coming in and playing with the FSN system in the living room. That would be a perfect press image and demonstrate that the system was real. Neighbors could object to the parking, so traffic would have to be managed.

There was a long list of tasks, but Benya was undaunted. He met Levin's gaze and gave him an impish smile. "Sure, we'll be ready."

Benya got on the phone that night and sounded the alarm to the contractors in charge. The next morning, battalions of trucks and vans descended on the house, pouring out workers to handle wiring, installations, decorations, and landscaping. The lead contractor, a World War II veteran, told Benya, "I haven't seen this much activity since D-Day."

The NOC was filled with a sense of excitement, masking an underlying current of dread. The apps were coming along, providing the opportunity to show the world things that had never been seen before. But the network itself was fragile and prone to breakdowns. The engineers were experiencing something that even the most casual computer user knows when it comes to digital products: Sometimes things go wrong for no apparent reason.

Software engineers toiled through a list of 500 to 600 "known bugs," only to continually find unknown ones—the really big problems were dubbed "show stoppers." With three weeks left before launch, engineers said, the network was crashing about four out of every ten times it was booted up.

The developers tried to keep their sense of humor. As the launch neared, Ludington found Callahan hunched over monitors, nearly catatonic, and still wearing the same polo shirt he had on the day before. Ludington insisted that Callahan go home and get some sleep. Once he was gone, Ludington retuned all of Callahan's TV monitors to adult channels so that when Callahan returned, he got an eyeful of porn.

There was a rumor that at some point an engineer for one of the partner companies was found dead inside the NOC. But that remained unconfirmed, perhaps a product of FSN mythology.

The launch event, staged with the help of Broadstreet Productions, a New York production firm, would be on a scale that the industry had rarely seen. Planning it became "all-consuming," Luftman said. For the location, organizers selected a ballroom in a Sheraton Hotel off Interstate 4 due to its proximity to the NOC and Home of the 21st Century. The hotel also had space for exhibit booths to showcase technology partners and their digital ware.

Shortly before Thanksgiving, Time Warner's corporate PR managers came from New York to see what they would be promoting. The first time they got a demo, the network crashed.

"I was white. I thought *holy shit*," said Peter Quinn, Time Warner's corporate editorial director, who was working on Levin's launch speech. He had visions of an embarrassing catastrophe. "We'll be on a bus with hats pulled over our ears, trying to get out of Orlando."

The enormity of demonstrating an unproven, unreliable network was dawning on everyone. "This was live," stressed Time Warner PR executive Tod Hullin. "There wasn't any tape to rerun. If it didn't work, we were going to embarrass ourselves in front of the world."

"It was December fourteenth, right?" said Rick Colletto, an FSN VOD manager. "We weren't sure there was going to be a December fifteenth if the network didn't boot up while Jim and Jerry were up there."

I CAN'T REALLY RECALL WHY, but I flew to Orlando to join the press corps for the launch event. It might have turned out to be like a journey to Mecca, or it could've been a trip on the Titanic. Amid all the struggles of digital ventures in those days, it would've been nice to see something that actually had some merit. But the hype meter in my head was clicking slowly, like a metronome.

I joined a press corps of some 300 US and international journalists who descended on the Sheraton. It was an outdated hotel with worn-out bowed mattresses, so I didn't sleep well (the hotel has since been renovated). When December 14 dawned, overcast and gray, I was in no mood for a parade of hyperbole.

Inside the Sheraton ballroom, technicians were positioning lights and checking microphones on the ballroom stage. The stage set and props resembled a living room, with two seats at center stage in front of a widescreen projector screen. Off to one side was a six-foot-tall mockup of a TV remote control with the words Time Warner across the top of it. Today, photos of the remote make it appear ordinary because the design was utilized in millions of TV remotes that followed.

Levin, in his quintessential dark suit, stepped onto the stage with his PR handlers to check out the final arrangements. Dozens of top Time Warner officials and executives from partner companies were present. SGI media handlers, running around in clean white outfits, gave the event a New Age touch. Their cheery disposition made my hype meter rattle, but I was so fascinated by what was going on that I decided not to pass judgment yet.

In addition to the ballroom gala, the hotel's Azalea Room contained an exhibit floor that offered a glimpse of future interactive services, including an exhibit for HBO On Demand, the first revelation of a subscription video-on-demand service that would launch years later. Time Warner also reached into its media properties to showcase a prototype Sports Illustrated TV service. (In 1996 the company launched CNN/SI, a twenty-four-hour sports news network, but amid a crowded market for sports news, it lasted less than six years.)

Another marvel prominently on the exhibit floor was the presence of rock musician Todd Rundgren, who was fronting a nascent music service. Rundgren's songs include plaintive tunes like "Hello It's Me," psychedelic rock, and the party romp "Bang the Drum All Day." He displayed a personal fascination for interactive entertainment. Looking every bit like a rock star, he wore blond highlights in his hair, dark sunglasses, a red-and-black plaid suit, and high-top sneakers.

Most of the engineers in the NOC had pulled an all-nighter.

During the final run-throughs, the network crashed once again, making their coffee-filled stomachs churn. The Sheraton posed an additional technical challenge because engineers had to rely upon coaxial cable that was used internally for the hotel's master antenna TV system that supplied TV service for guests. Feige said the coax was "leakier than a sieve."

The engineers had readied the Oh Jesus Switch, which would trigger a backup network in the event that the main network failed, and a substitute demo on disc. But what if even those didn't work?

Nearby at the Home of the 21st Century, developers worked late into the night to put the finishing touches on the house. The infinite strands of wires to connect all of the gadgets were being stuffed everywhere—underneath rugs, behind furniture, and throughout the attic.

Michael Adams watched a worker jamming wires into a credenza, like he was an Italian chef filling a bowl with pasta. Adams remembers being "quite unpopular" with the Atari team when he had to disconnect their game console from an HCT because the lone printer port was needed for an HP printer to print coupons—"just hours before the launch event!"

Tensions were running high. As zero hour approached, workers were filling up the pool, arranging furniture, and rolling out sod.

IT WAS TIME FOR THE event to begin. I sat in front of the stage with the other reporters, my pen and notebook ready to record whatever may come. Standing in the back of the room were dozens of FSN employees, PR people, and executives from participating companies.

Levin was ready. Nearly twenty years earlier, he celebrated the satellite launch of HBO in Vero Beach, FL. Now he was back in Florida for what he hoped would be another triumph.

FSN was going to launch with only five user sites—a small step toward 4,000 homes—but nobody would really care as long as the network held up. Luftman said, "The message we were delivering was this: It's here, it's real, it works, and it's spectacular."

Yet the project was being given a different PR spin compared to the January 1993 announcement, when Levin stated that it was not a test but an actual service launch. Executives had toned down the rhetoric and couched FSN as a trial. Chiddix and others labeled FSN as a "time machine," a glimpse into the future to see what an interactive system would look like and what consumers would purchase.

The press didn't buy it. Prior to the launch event, reporters chastised Time Warner for its waffling. *The New York Times* chided, "This is a test. This is only a test. It is not—repeat, *not*—the interactive television and home-shopping system that will be in your home by Christmas. Or next Christmas. Or maybe ever."

An Associated Press report said, "Hyped and bashed, interactive TV is getting another moment in the sun—Florida's to be exact. . . . Although the company won't discuss money, the project is believed to cost in the tens of millions of dollars and be the nation's most expensive interactive TV experiment." *BusinessWeek* said, "Interactive television, at long last, is here. Sort of. Well, at least part of it." The industry trades were not much kinder. *Inside Media* said, "What's most notable is what's not on the service that was originally billed as the broadband interactive TV of the future." *MediaWeek* added that "other new-media players assert FSN is either economically unrealistic, technologically misguided, or both."

As the hour of reckoning arrived, the ballroom was full of nervous energy. Feige took a seat in the front row. An event organizer had presented him with a statue of Alfred E. Neuman, *Mad* magazine's iconic figure whose slogan was "What, me worry?" because Feige appeared to be so calm. Inside, he wasn't feeling calm at all.

Callahan took his place behind the stage set and strapped on his microphone headset. His normal good humor was being sorely tested by sleep deprivation.

Ludington, Williamson, Kanouff, and other members of the team were ensconced in the NOC. "I remember feeling immense pressure to have it work," Kanouff said.

Everything was as ready as it could be. They could pull this off, provided that the transmissions held up and the computers didn't crash and the server spit out the right movie and the switches didn't lock up and the Sheraton didn't sink into the swamp.

To increase their odds, the engineers switched off all of the HCT boxes at demonstration sites around the hotel and Home of the 21st Century so that the entire network was serving just the one box that was on stage. Feige recalls there was a brief moment of panic when engineers discovered that a Sheraton chambermaid had flipped on a box in the hotel and started fooling around with it.

Joe Collins stepped onto the stage, made some opening remarks, and introduced Levin. Speaking forcefully, Levin said, "Sooner or later, every significant player in the information and entertainment industry is going to have to understand the implications of broadband interactivity and, far more important, to design the programming and services that match the special abilities of the medium and the special expectations of those who use it." He touted Time Warner's lead in the race to interactivity and said it was the best-positioned company to deploy the digital architecture.

"The pressure of imposing a public deadline—of challenging ourselves to have the FSN up and running—has produced its share of headaches," Levin said. "Everyone who's worked on this project has come to feel the excitement of being part of an enterprise whose effects go far beyond what happens here today. We understand that the introduction of the FSN into the first American homes is an irreversible step across the threshold of change. A step away from the world as it is to what it will be."

The audience was subjected to a panel of executives from the key tech suppliers, including SGI, S-A, AT&T, and Hewlett-Packard. Everyone had to get their photo op. The execs cited factors such as hybrid fiber-coaxial architecture, ATM switching, server advances, and Moore's law as the foundations for the project. SGI's McCracken surprised observers by declaring that a $300 set-top was achievable by the end of 1995.

SGI's engineers had learned some crucial differences between the TV and PC, McCracken told the audience. "Our software designers learned that interactive television doesn't work with an interface that's built from the conventions of computing. We learned that we had to respect the way people watch television and use remote controls today. The team also learned that people don't want to read television. Therefore, a PC-style point-and-click, text and icon approach is trouble," he said.

"Television is about sound and motion and kinetics, a constant stream of information. Our living room tests revealed some unexpected results. We discovered that the interface had to be transparent, in the same way you use a doorknob. There's no thought as to how to operate the doorknob; you just do it. The Silicon Graphics team invented what amounts to a full-motion, dynamic, kinetic, transparent doorknob that opens the door to a new form of human activity."

Despite that interesting concession about television from a Silicon Valley leader, the speakers' remarks were getting interminably long, the air was getting sucked out of the room, and the suspense kept building. I was getting fidgety. *When are they going to turn it on?*

Levin and Chiddix walked toward their seats in front of a widescreen TV while the audience watched on the giant projection screen. "This is not a hollow demonstration. This is not hype. We're on the cable system," Levin explained. "There are no animals behind here on roller skates," he said, eliciting nervous laughter from the audience.

Chiddix picked up the FSN remote. The plan was for Chiddix to press the remote to start FSN's on-screen Carousel program navigator, then show off the rest of the service. The engineers had asked that a demonstration script be drawn up so they knew precisely where Chiddix would go and could ensure the network would show something once he got there.

Jim Ludington talked to Jim Chiddix and Jerry Levin via a closed-circuit feed moments before the service launch (photo courtesy of Jim Ludington and Laura Nolte).

Before pressing the button, the executives checked in with Ludington via a brief interview using a closed-circuit video feed with the NOC. Looking like an anglo-fied Geraldo Rivera, Ludington raced hurriedly through the NOC, pointing at equipment and throwing in technical terms that either fascinated the reporters or confused them. Either response was fine as long as the press realized how complex this was.

Then Levin surprised Ludington by asking what he personally thought of the service. Ludington froze, staring into the camera. His mind seemed to go blank, perhaps distracted by the enormity of the moment and the activity swirling around him. Then he remembered why he was there. He remembered that his mom had produced *The Howdy Dowdy Show* and his dad worked for ABC-TV, and now he was part of the next generation of television. He didn't say it quite the way he wanted, but he got the point across.

That done, it was showtime. Chiddix aimed the remote. "Well, Jerry, let's just turn on our television and . . ." Levin sat forward in his seat and clasped his hands together. He looked anxious. A swarm of photographers crowded the stage and focused their cameras on the two executives.

Ludington and the team inside the NOC watched intently on monitors. *Come on, come on, make it work.*

Chiddix pushed the button and a blue-and-white FSN logo came onto the giant screen. Suddenly, there was loud, swirling music that shook the ballroom, and the screen filled with a whirling mass of colorful shapes that spiraled upward and formed into the Carousel on-screen navigator. The Carousel, with happy music, turned to offer movies, shopping, games. It was bright, colorful, captivating. It worked!

Thunderous applause and cheers erupted from the back of the ballroom. A sense of elation and relief was palpable. The wave of applause washed over me, and the hairs rose on the back of my neck. The FSN employees, partners, and PR professionals were cheering, the executives around the room applauded, and the reporters joined right in. "That was the damndest thing I'd ever seen," a PR executive said of the reporters' response.

I was trying to take notes, but my hand was shaking from a rush of adrenaline. It felt like we were witnessing history, but what exactly was happening? I thought, *Are we about to see the face of God?*

Inside the NOC, there were a lot of goosebumps and sighs of relief. Ludington said, "After all of the nightmares and all of the battles and the negotiations and the long days and the traveling, to have that music come up and the Carousel start, it . . . it was like you went unconscious almost. That was spine-*ting*-ling. It was huge, it was huge."

Daniel Levy is among those who compare that moment to the births of their children. Bill Brown, the TWC division president who'd struggled with corporate management and the engineers, recalled, "I had tears in my eyes. I'm serious. It made you very proud to be part of the company."

Levin agreed. "I would have to say, regardless of what the postmortems are on the Full Service Network, to be up there with Chiddix and turn the service on and have the Carousel come up, that was, emotionally, one of the most exciting moments of my life."

Okay, so the network turned on. Now what could it do? Chiddix started clicking through the navigation guide. Beside him, Levin watched intently. The reporters moved forward in their seats. Lindsay overheard one reporter gasping to another, "This is history in the making, this is history in the making."

Chiddix spun the Carousel and showed off the different application venues, each fronted with colorful, high-tech graphics. It looked so good that there was an excitement bordering on giddiness. The network was holding up, the machines humming along. Everyone was riveted.

"Uh-oh, what's going on?"

Callahan recalled hearing those alarming words coming through his headset from an engineer watching on a monitor inside the NOC. Callahan peered onto the stage and saw the reason for concern. *What the . . .*

Levin was reaching out his hand, about to take the remote from Chiddix. Levin was clearly about to go off script. Who knew where he would go and what it might do to the network.

"Now, Jim," Levin said, "how about if I try and use the system?"

"Sure," Chiddix replied, looking green. But after all, Levin had footed the bill for all this. It was Levin's show. Chiddix handed him the remote.

"Jerry's got the remote," Callahan said, breathing into his mike. *Oh shit*, he thought. They'd thought of everything but this. The whole demo was in danger of collapsing because of one of the simplest of all truths: Guys like to control the TV remote.

Panic spread around the NOC and the ballroom. Engineers hovered over the Oh Jesus Switch. "Everybody was freaking out," Williamson recalled with a laugh.

Levin clicked rapidly through the on-demand movie venue while Chiddix watched intently. Levin scrolled through some movie trailers, then ordered *The Specialist*, starring Sylvester Stallone and Sharon Stone, a recent Warner Bros. theatrical release.

The movie popped right up and began playing. Levin used the Fast Forward function to skip through the movie in ten-minute increments, lightning fast. *Whoa*, gasped the audience, applauding more. Nobody had ever seen that capability before. It was magical. Seeing a streamed movie handled with on-demand functions for the first time was like silent movies going to talkies or Dorothy stepping from black-and-white into Munchkinland Technicolor. This was a game changer.

Levin made jokes while everyone in the NOC was sweating bullets, waiting for the network to crash. He paused the movie at precisely a point where Sharon Stone was placing a flower on a grave. Then he ordered a second movie, *The Client*, and paused that too. So now two movies were being held on the network simultaneously. It was a first, but it essentially doubled the chances that the network would crash.

Levin handed the remote back to Chiddix, which only marginally relieved the engineers' angst. Chiddix used the remote to access the shopping app and fly into the virtual shopping mall. He went into the Warner Bros. store, where Bugs Bunny provided a cheery video greeting. It was a great mix of high-tech graphics and old-school cartoons. Warner Bros., which initially resisted FSN, now looked like the star of the show.

Levin told Chiddix to order a pair of $10 raspberry-colored Bugs Bunny caps. Nearby, a Hewlett-Packard printer spewed out their order confirmation.

Backstage, every move was breathlessly reported through the headset mikes: "He's buying the hats. . . . He bought the hats."

Next, Chiddix showed how 64-bit Atari Jaguar games could be downloaded through the network in a venue called PlayWay. It featured an animated character, SkateKid, who rode a skateboard and wore an oversized red sweatshirt and a yellow-and-red beanie, although inexplicably, he had no mouth or nose. Anyway, it was apparently an attempt to show that the service could appeal to 1990s slackers.

To demonstrate how games could be played across the network, Chiddix introduced the audience to America's first FSN family: the Willards—Karl and Susan Willard and their son Brad and daughter Jaclyn—a local family who'd been tucked away in Ludington's office and now appeared before the audience on the big screen, grinning at the camera. The family played interactive gin rummy against Levin and Chiddix, a cute moment that thankfully ended before it revealed that digital activity can be just as dull as real life. There was a momentary, heart-stopping glitch in the on-screen video, but technicians later blamed it on the closed-circuit feed, not the network.

Now, Levin announced, he was tired and wanted to return to watching his first movie, *The Specialist*, if the network remembered where he left off.

Through his headset, Callahan could hear yelling inside the NOC: "Check the server! Check the server!" Was the movie still there?

Chiddix clicked the remote, and up popped Sharon Stone, still bent over the grave. The audience applauded. "Oh, thank God," Callahan gasped. It felt like days since they'd left that movie behind.

Amid the applause, Levin waved his hand toward the screen in triumph. "To me, the system is worth it, just for this."

The network held up. Levin had gone out on a tightrope and glided back safely. The engineers were breathing again. Levin was a hero. They were all heroes. "We were all very proud afterward," Kanouff said.

Later, it became known that the night before the launch event, Levin and the PR people had agreed that he should take control of the remote and show how easy it was to work the network. But apparently, the engineers never got the word.

The demo ended, and the press headed off to tour the facilities, including the NOC, exhibit booths, Digital Production Center, and Home of the 21st Century. Outside, the clouds were breaking and the sun was bursting through.

The network, despite heavy usage, held up throughout the day. It worked so smoothly that several skeptical reporters demanded to know what was happening behind the walls, as if there really were animals on roller skates.

■ ▶ ▶▶

"WELCOME TO THE HOME OF the 21st Century." On a large monitor, Alfred, a computer-animated butler named after the Batman character, greeted visitors to the modern house. They were about to see Benya's handiwork.

In the living room, the Willard's son played with the FSN apps on a large TV while news photographers snapped away. A Honeywell home automation system handled lighting, thermostat, and other controls. Alfred, a bespectacled cartoon face, could be programmed to oversee house functions and greetings, including, "Chip, chip, cheerio! Wake up and smell the coffee!" Other gadgetry was placed around the home. The house quickly became packed with visitors and press, many still buzzing about the launch event they'd just witnessed.

Soon, the whole world knew what Time Warner had accomplished. The press cynicism completely flipped. Reuters dashed off a wire story: "Media Giant Launches Cable Network of Future." *USA Today* declared, "The future of television landed in a tired-looking Sheraton outside Orlando on Wednesday." *The New York Times* said Time Warner put on a "glittering display of its vision for television in the future."

"Media's new baby born in Orlando," heralded the *Denver Post*. *Time* magazine called FSN "the Cadillac of interactive-TV tests—and surprisingly fun to drive." A columnist for *Telephony* noted that the VOD quality and functionality was superior to a VCR and concluded, "Seeing the FSN in action was thrilling." In Orlando, where FSN was getting so much local attention, the *Orlando Sentinel* reported, "The national hoopla surrounding the public debut of Time Warner Cable's television system of the future is over, but for 4,000 Central Florida homes, the era of interactive TV is just beginning." All of the major evening newscasts ran stories.

Tom Southwick, editor of the trade publication *Cable World*, compared Orlando to Kitty Hawk, writing, "If Orville and Wilbur Wright were making their historic first airplane flight today . . . the press would've pointed out that the brothers' first effort was postponed due to bad winds; that construction of the plane was months behind schedule; and there was no real proof that consumers would ever be willing to pay to fly in an airplane because everyone already had access to good train and boat service where you could sit on a seat instead of lie on your belly. . . . What the skeptics fail to grasp is that the elegant and user-friendly system that Time Warner showed December 14 is the most primitive and clumsy and least-efficient version of the FSN that'll ever exist."

I wrote a column for *Cablevision* saying that video-on-demand appeared to be the big winner while the success of the interactive services remained to be seen. In short, I waffled appropriately.

The Willards were media stars in newspaper stories and TV reports around the world. They spent the day—and the next two-and-a-half years—getting peppered with questions about how they liked FSN. "I took media to the Willards' home multiple times a week for interviews. Finally, we brought in other families so we could give them a break," Lindsay said.

"We had no idea what we were getting into," Susan Willard told me with a laugh. *The New York Times* ran a Sunday feature story that began "Meet the Willards. For at least one day last week, they were America's most popular TV family." After the launch, the Willards wrote a letter to Levin thanking him for their involvement and hailing FSN as a godsend for America's families.

Many investment firms issued positive comments and "buy" recommendations for Time Warner as well as its vendor partners. Goldman Sachs & Co. said it was "impressed with the user friendliness of the system," and it "points to exciting opportunities." Oppenheimer & CO. called it "quite impressive" and Alex. Brown & Sons said it has "an awesome remote control, worth fighting for." Raymond Katz of Bear Stearns Companies, Inc., said, "We confess to being impressed with what we saw." Tom Wolzien of Bernstein said "a significant and comprehensible new strategy is emerging" involving FSN and Time Warner's internet interest. The biggest questions, analysts generally agreed, involved timing and costs.

Despite the heavy media coverage, Peter Quinn believed, "The press didn't match what happened in the room that day." (Quinn went on to become a bestselling novelist and historian.)

The evening after the launch, once all the reporters left, the FSN crew gathered at the Home of the 21st Century for a blowout victory party. Levin and the other main players showed up. The house was teeming with revelers. Then people started jumping or getting shoved into the pool. Callahan reported, "A lot of tension got released that night." Chiddix, in his low, melodic tone, stated, "Hijinks ensued."

But Feige was subdued. His wife had called. She informed Tom that his father had died. The man who'd raised Tom in an orderly Midwestern home, served for years at IBM, and had given his son the character to get people to work together for a common good, was gone. In a single day, Feige experienced one of the highest points of his professional life and the lowest point in his personal life. While happy for his team, he said, "That sort of took the wind out of my personal sails."

Levin summed up the day: "It was a tremendously emotional event." Indeed, he had pulled off a feat worthy of Prometheus. He brought fire to Orlando.

Bob Benya and Jim Ludington ended up in the pool during the post-launch celebration (photo courtesy of Jim Ludington).

CHAPTER 11
KEEPING UP WITH THE WILLARDS

The Willard family, including son Brad, became FSN media darlings (*Multichannel News*).

FSN MADE A DAZZLING DEBUT, but it was running in only five sites, a far cry from the 4,000 home target. It was still more like a prototype than a commercial service. Although Levin initially positioned FSN as an actual service, media handlers dubbed it "the world's first digital interactive television trial" in press materials, according to Lindsay.

Reporters continued to hover over the project. "At our peak, we were handling up to fifty calls a day from media around the world," Lindsay said. Due to reporters' inquiries and requests for tours, "I had to hire a team of ten people just to help keep up with the demand," she said.

Due to the high expectations, the press grew skeptical again. "Three months after a splashy demonstration of its Full Service Network, Time Warner Cable has only about a dozen users getting movies and video games," the AP reported. The *Orlando Sentinel* appeared to turn on its interactive news partner. "Full Service Network Not Close To Full Speed," a headline said. "Half of the year is now up, and from all outward appearances, the company has made little progress. The system has been expanded to just '30-plus' subscribers. . . . And no major new services, such as news on demand or banking by TV, have been added. Still, a sampling of subscribers found them to be enthusiastic about the system and eager—in a few cases, impatient—for more services."

By fall, an AP headline stated, "Time Warner Experiment, At Last, Begins Expansion." The article said, "After a slow and sometimes frustrating ten months, Time Warner Cable's high profile experiment in two-way TV is finally rolling out to a broad number of homes. . . . In the past few weeks, with new software completed and several other difficulties resolved, Time Warner technicians have been attaching new customers in several suburbs north of Orlando at a rate approaching 40 a day. By this weekend, nearly 500 homes were hooked up."

During the launch event, the VOD movies worked flawlessly. But delivering multiple movies into the neighborhoods added an extra dimension. Early on, outages and glitches were commonplace, according to the engineers. But on-demand movies proved their allure, attracting customers and gaining interest from Hollywood studios.

"After the public launch, other studios signed up after meeting with us in Orlando to view demonstrations and learn about our technical distribution architecture and security protocols," Benya said. "I recall Universal being an early content partner, which helped with others coming on board."

Movies-on-demand proved to be the killer application that Time Warner was looking for. It provided the convenience and magic that consumers desired. Various prices for movies were tested—$2.95, $3.95, and $4.95 for new releases, $1.95 for classic films—and any price received uptake, according to application managers. Research showed that consumers clearly felt that VOD was more convenient than going to the video store.

"To me, the biggest gem was the intensive use of movies-on-demand," Levin said. Like Christopher Columbus sailing for the Far East but running into the Americas, the developers went on a grand voyage to discover interactive TV and instead found the treasure of movie streaming.

FSN typically offered about sixty titles at a time, which managers came to believe was all that was needed for VOD, largely a hit-driven business. In addition to *The Fugitive*, popular movies included *The Pelican Brief*, *Point of No Return*, *Free Willy*, *Dave*, *Sommersby*, and *Man Without a Face*, according to Benya. The licensing deals were similar to PPV, with studios typically getting a 40 percent revenue share, he said.

Since the number of households was small, the studios primarily used FSN as a learning lab. VOD achieved buy rates that were several times higher than PPV, which was both a blessing and a curse. While heralding a new revenue source, VOD fed studio concerns that it would cannibalize home video revenue.

Later, FSN on-demand offerings, under the banner of Custom TV, included Soap Operas on Demand and archives of *The Ed Sullivan Show* and *Monty Python's Flying Circus*. Sports Illustrated TV struck deals with the National Football League and National Basketball Association to enable customers to call up scores and player statistics during games, as well as access to videos such as *NFL Bloopers*. Through a Smart Living on-screen venue, viewers could access children's videos (titles such as *Big Bird Sings*), lifestyle (*Living Fully Until Death*), history (*Secrets of the Titanic*), and computer education (*Introduction to Windows 3.1*).

With the advent of on-demand streaming, the engineers began to tackle a mathematical calculation faced by network engineers for years to follow. It was sometimes referred to as the Mother's Day Conundrum, but technically it's known as peak concurrency. For years on Mother's Day, millions of people called their moms, which could overload telephone networks and disrupt service. Similarly, if a streaming service gets overloaded from too much demand, users see a spinning wheel, the modern equivalent of a telephone busy signal.

But if technicians overengineered their networks and accounted for a high level of demand that went unfulfilled, it equated to an expensive waste of server space and other technology. In the early days of VOD, TWC and Comcast engineered their systems for a peak concurrency of 10 percent, accounting for one-tenth of their subscribers simultaneously using the service. But, according to former executives from both companies, that level turned out to be too high. They don't recall concurrency ever going above mid single digits.

A YEAR AFTER THE PUBLIC launch, FSN was finally ready to serve the total 4,000-home target area. In a December 1995 report to TWC in Stamford, Tom Feige stated, "The great technology news of the month is that for the first time in television entertainment history, the world's first interactive digital broadband network was completely operational with all designed components effectively serving subscribers. All eight servers and associated vaults, ATM switch and RF, and optical network components are currently in the operating cluster and began serving subscribers in all sixteen neighborhoods this month."

The lessons of early interactive TV began to take shape. Amid skepticism that anyone would interact with their TV set, people did interact. Every application that FSN offered—customized news and information, time-shifted soap operas, sports statistics, at-home banking—found an audience. According to managers, apps usually achieved penetration of 10 percent or more of FSN customers.

"We learned there was consumer demand for this stuff, and I

think that was the most important lesson," Rossetti told me in an interview later.

FSN provided a thorough market test of interactivity by recording every remote click by users, sometimes up to three-quarters of a million a day, managers said. Data was required to be collected on an anonymous basis and couldn't be shared with third parties because cable providers lived under tight privacy restrictions established in the 1992 Cable Act.

Next to VOD, interactive games proved to be popular with adults and kids, despite stiff competition from games for PCs and game devices. Under the PlayWay banner, FSN offered Atari Jaguar games that could be downloaded to a 64-bit player. In-network games, including classic card and board games, were developed by SGI for the set-top and allowed for multiple players—up to four for a game called TVBots. Plans to include the Sega Channel, the game download service that had backing from TCI and Time Warner Cable, were discussed, but former managers do not recall that it was deployed.

Many neighbors regularly played games across the network and, after a free trial, paid a per-day or per-month fee. Games users were "a hardcore group," said games director Scott Hochgesang. Solitaire was the most popular game, he said, while networked games brought neighbors together. One group played gin rummy every day, sometimes up to three hours a day, he recalled.

"We had an amazing roster of games running in the test labs that did not get to customers. It was very difficult developing fun games on an SGI workstation platform that was very hard to code on," Hochgesang said.

It's a well-recited fact that the most popular shopping application was ordering stamps from the post office, to the surprise of almost everyone. With a click of their remote, subscribers could buy stamps and a postal employee would deliver them the next day. FSN had tapped into the convenience factor. The concept was later expanded online through Stamps.com, which enables people to print US postage stamps.

FSN users could order from Pizza Hut without having to go to the phone. Through the app, they could select different toppings for their pie. It was popular, but later it created a negative connotation for the entire project. Detractors said Time Warner spent all that money just to learn that people like pizza.

In an in-home banking app, Barnett Bank customers could be served by a virtual teller in the form of a golden retriever or a bear. Customers could access their accounts, transfer funds, and get loan and service information.

The interactive shopping mall didn't fare as well. Despite its high-tech look and inclusion of top stores Crate & Barrel, Spiegel, Best Buy, and Sharper Image, the application was slow and frustrating.

"It was hard to use, it wasn't fluid, it wasn't facile. Besides, people weren't buying it anyhow," Levin said.

FSN developers explored other innovations that weren't deployed on the system. Decades before grocery delivery services, they tested grocery store shopping using technology from CUC International, operated by a company called ShopperVision. Viewers could enter a virtual grocery store, pull a product off the shelf, turn the product to check the content label, and then purchase it. According to a YouTube video posted by developer Sandy Goldman, ShopperVision customers could go to a virtual checkout counter and be greeted by a video of Robin Leach, TV host of *Lifestyles of the Rich and Famous*. The service posed many operational challenges that weren't resolved until years later by online grocery services.

Ralph Brown, who had a degree in speech recognition technology, studied the concept of voice-controlled TV remotes. The technical and operational means were prohibitive then; today voice-controlled remotes are ubiquitous.

FSN tested an internet-on-TV service called WebLink, which used a virtual on-screen keyboard and search function. It gained some traction, largely with those who didn't have internet access or a computer, managers recalled. The company learned an important lesson long before others did: Ultimately, putting the web on TV is not a satisfying experience. Microsoft purchased WebTV and pushed the concept (so did Time Warner's future partner, AOL, with AOL TV). WebTV also gained popularity, mainly with people who didn't own PCs, but the allure faded, and WebTV was shuttered in 2013.

Walter Isaacson, who'd pushed Levin toward the internet, recognized what others later would repeat. In a 1998 interview, he told me, "The TV is something you watch from ten feet away, and it doesn't talk back to you. The PC, you sit a foot away and get information from it."

When it came to interactivity, Ludington said, "Lean-forward technology won over lean back."

MEANWHILE, IN LOS ANGELES, WARNER Bros. was digitizing films, and the Home Video division was interested in distributing them on discs. With Toshiba, which held a small ownership stake in Time Warner, the company pioneered the invention of the DVD. Movies on discs extended the life of Warner Home Video in the face of VOD. Warren Lieberfarb, the division president who is said to have resisted VOD to save home video profits, was heralded as the father of the DVD.

The technical underpinnings of DVDs began at FSN. "All that work was the predecessor to creating the DVD," Kanouff said. "That wasn't what we were trying to do, but we ended up creating a digital storage and playout medium for every person in their home."

Chris Cookson, who served as president of technical operations and CTO for Warner Bros. at the time, said, "DVD grew directly out of the Full Service Network. You can see exactly how the DVD was a descendant of FSN, because we did the movies there and took the expertise we gained from that to the development of the DVD."

Warner Bros. also used its digital experience to extend the reach of its nascent WB Network, a broadcast network owned by Warner

Bros. and the Tribune Company, headed by Jamie Kellner. To reach the smallest 100 US markets, where it lacked network affiliates, Warner Bros. beamed a satellite feed of the national network to cable headends. There, an IBM computer equipped with content on a disk drive stitched in commercials and promos to fit the local market. Cable operators could carry the so-called WB 100+ for free.

"We used satellite to deliver all of it; then we used PCs to put it all back together so when it played out, it looked like a network affiliate," Cookson said. "So FSN begat the DVD, which begat the WB 100+, which became the basis for how you do digital distribution."

Warner Bros. retained ownership of patents for DVDs, which became the next popular form of home video after videocassettes. The DVD format was first introduced in Japan in 1996 and Warner Home Video released the first titles in the US in early 1997, according to a Wikipedia history. Sales of DVD players grew throughout the late 1990s and surpassed VCR sales in 2001. In the early 2000s, DVD disc sales and rentals were a $20-billion-plus annual business. That was until Netflix began streaming in 2007 and eventually sent home video spiraling downward.

IN ORLANDO, MANY FSN CUSTOMERS enjoyed being the first on their block to have the latest thing. In addition to the Willards, several other families became media stars, including Jody Weiss and her family.

One TV writer reported, "When it comes to watching TV, Jody Weiss and her kids are living like the Jetsons." Weiss noted the international interest by checking a bulletin board full of business cards and saying, "We've had people from Germany, Japan, Norway, Sweden, and all across the country."

Still, others had to be persuaded to sign up for FSN. Once again, Benya worked his marketing magic. His staff set up a Marketing War Room that plotted strategy and produced promo campaigns.

Inside the FSN Marketing War Room (photo courtesy of Laura Nolte).

To attract customers, marketers used an acquisition process that Benya termed a "velvet touch." The process involved direct mail, telemarketing, and door-to-door sales. Once signed up, customers were given a welcome kit and an "FSN happy hour gourmet lunch" while an installation was made, which could take about two hours.

The staff developed an FSN University to train new employees, who received background materials in notebooks that had a metallic high-tech cover. Retention efforts included a monthly FSN magazine, bill inserts, mailers, and digitized on-air spots. FSN also took care to assuage expressed consumer concerns over potentially higher bills, privacy issues, and a possible "dehumanizing effect" from interactivity.

FSN became a mecca for "executives, politicians, and royalty," Benya said. More than 14,000 people toured the NOC and Home of the 21st Century, according to Lindsay. A house tour cost $5, part of which went to charity. Many visitors came from foreign countries to see the latest American marvel.

An FSN demo site was established at Disney's Epcot Center. Benya's marketing machine ordered FSN-branded souvenirs, including baseball caps, ties, pens, and Frisbees. Visitors to Orlando could return home with Mickey Mouse ears and an FSN cap.

CHAPTER 12
THE FEWEST CLICKS WINS

On screen, the Carousel navigator spun to display interactive services (photo courtesy of Laura Nolte).

W<small>HAT WAS IT THAT</small> drew people to on-demand video and interactive media and, in many cases, pay for it?

"We came up with this concept of 'choice, control, and convenience,'" Feige said. "In hindsight, I'd say it probably should have been 'convenience, convenience, and convenience.' Choice is also somewhat of an important consideration, but not nearly as important as convenience. In the longer run, as we move to larger networks, obviously, choice is an important element. But it wasn't as important as we originally thought it was going to be."

FSN's convenience displayed itself in many forms: the convenience of ordering movies when you wanted; playing games with friends remotely; and shopping from your living room. Benya said convenience came to be the most important element to stress in FSN promotional materials.

The developers learned valuable lessons about user interfaces, usability, and navigation that web designers, apps developers, and streaming designers still grapple with today. They learned about the need for simplicity and easy accessibility to content. Television isn't a computer and shouldn't be treated as such. It shouldn't require layers of screens and multiple clicks. Nor should it overwhelm viewers with an overabundance of choices, a common mistake with early ITV services and even streaming services today. Interactivity requires that viewers get what they want as fast as they can. My favorite mantra that came out of the early designs was this: The fewest clicks wins. It meant that a UI should provide convenient access to content with the fewest number of clicks of a remote or touch pad possible. It's an ode to simplicity. I believe I first heard the phrase from Stephen Johnson, a user experience consultant for TWC and other companies.

The need for simple navigation became clear with the Carousel navigator. It may have looked cutting-edge, but it became an impediment to getting quick access to the applications. Users had to click their remote to turn on the Carousel and see it spin, then click on the genre they wanted, be it movies, games, or shopping, and then click to enter the venue and find their content. Too many clicks. Viewers could bypass the Carousel by entering the venue number on their remote, and they did.

For many homes, the Carousel was replaced by an interface called Omnio, a matrix showing numbered buttons for more direct access to content. By clicking number 1 for movies, a viewer could access a synopsis and poster image, an early example of VOD and streaming guides that followed.

While the goal was simplicity, the outcome for developers was complexity. A second TV remote had to be manufactured for Omnio, Levy recalled. He was responsible for style guides for the alternate interfaces, Carousel and Omnio. He said, "I often described that responsibility like this: making sure that FSN customers won't have to read an instruction manual in order to figure out how to watch TV."

What wasn't convenient was outages. In its early days, the network frequently crashed. Chiddix cited network reliability as the biggest challenge. Eventually, FSN said it established reliability on the order of 99 percent.

The company wasn't willing to give out much information about movie orders or other consumer usage, which fueled reporters and investors' frustration. Gary Arlen, a veteran journalist covering digital developments, said in a newsletter, "Unfortunately, the company won't say anything about buy rates at this point. 'It's really too soon to say with any statistical accuracy,' says Time Warner Cable spokesman John Dunn. 'But the preliminary information looks very good.' Still, the ITV technology, much of which was designed by Scientific Atlanta and Silicon Graphics, is suffering its share of technical difficulties, according to some subscribers. Some complain that services can be slow—and sometimes inaccessible."

FSN services were initially offered for free, and then the company attached a fee to just about everything, from $0.49 to play a game or watch *Monty Python* to tiers of content offered for free, $1.95, and $3.95. Such nickel and diming would never fly once the web came along and offered lots of content and social media for free, a practice that disrupted the models of traditional media companies like Time Warner. After that utopian exercise of "the internet wants to be free," both new media and traditional players tried to put the genie back in the bottle by setting up pay walls, ad-free pricing tiers, and other revenue-generating ploys. The practice continued as Netflix and other streaming services began offering customers more expensive subscription-only tiers and cheaper ad-supported options.

After the Omnio interface was introduced, FSN sent letters to customers saying it would charge $3.95 a month for it, essentially selling Omnio as a branded platform for on-demand and interactive fare. Omnio also included features designed to add to user convenience, including the ability to view your cable bill, learn about FSN applications, access a list of personal TV favorites, and link to capabilities such as ordering from Pizza Hut while watching a movie.

Reporting on the advent of Omnio, the *Orlando Sentinel* reported, "Some customers said they would gladly pay for the service, which most subscribers have had access to for 15 to 18 months. Others, though, complained about frustrating glitches that interrupted movies."

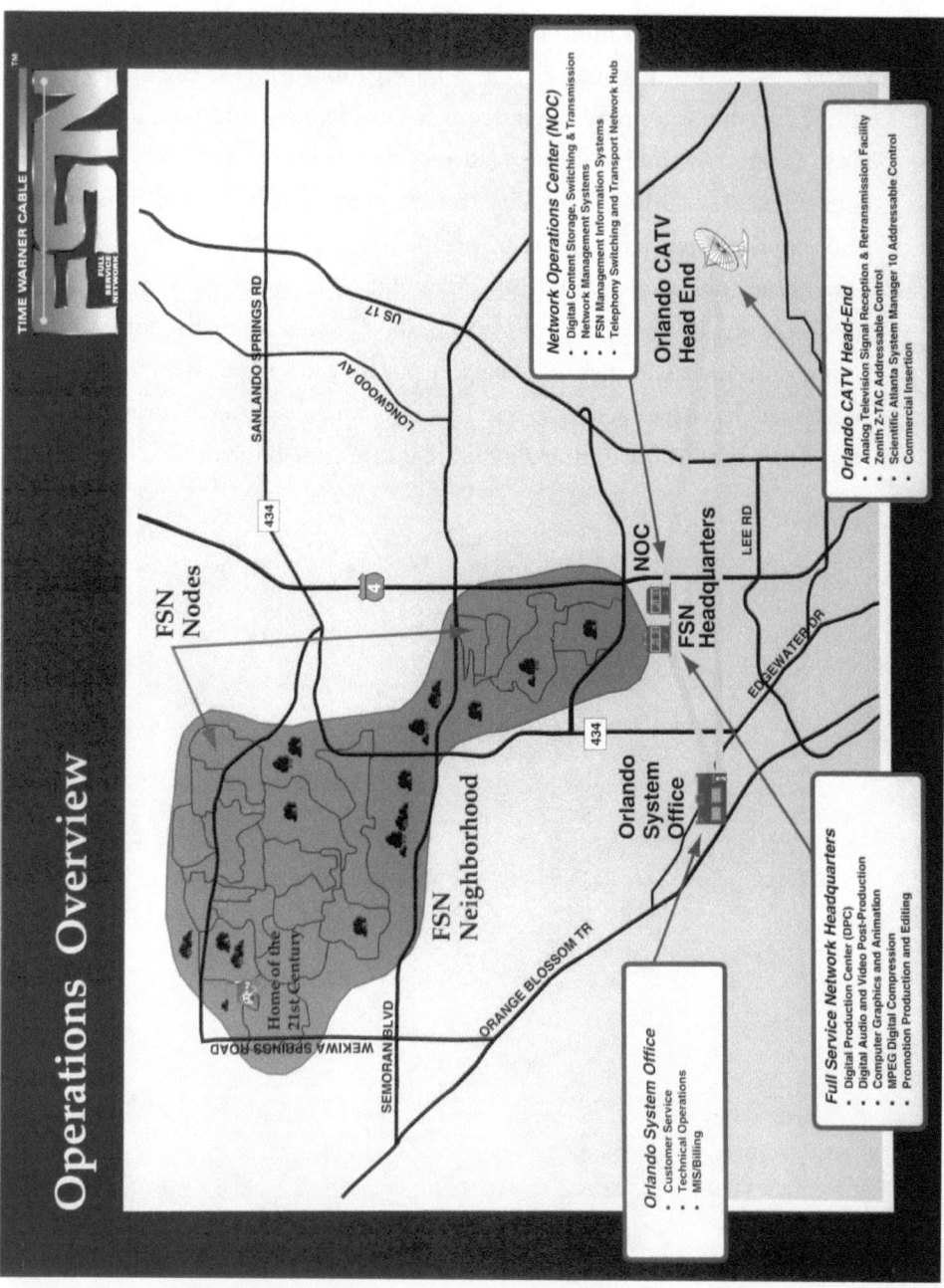

A map showing the FSN service area (photo courtesy of Barco Library, Syndeo Institute at The Cable Center).

CHAPTER 13
TIPPING THE SCALE

During FSN's heyday, Ludington was like a kid in a candy store. He was at the cable industry's epicenter for interactive apps development and state-of-the-art network engineering. It was a beehive of creativity, innovation, and positive vibes. Thousands of executives flocked to Orlando to tour the facility, and Ludington loved to show them the guts of the system, the refrigerator-sized servers, and other sizzling-hot equipment. But he also recognized that it was infeasible to roll out such an expensive network beyond the shadows of Disney World. And from the standpoint of interactive media, a greater force was taking over.

"The handwriting was on the wall," he said. "The blue-eyed baby turned out to be the internet."

Others were coming to the same conclusion. Cable executives were no longer debating whether the internet had a future; they were recognizing that the internet was the future. But how could a cable TV distribution network be used for the internet?

The 1995 Western Cable Show—the site where, three years earlier, Malone started a digital race in the cable industry—became a focal point for a change in the industry's thinking. "Many in the cable industry have changed channels to the internet and away from interactive television, but interactive TV isn't dead yet," *Multichannel News* reported. "At the Western Cable Show here, Time Warner Cable's Full Service Network officials still weren't saying where or when the service might be duplicated. They did unveil several potent, new interactive video services." Those services included the following: SITV with the NFL On Demand, TNX, Barnett Bank on-demand banking, GoTV shopping, Pizza Hut, and more games on the PlayWay. *MediaWeek* said FSN was becoming "the fuller service network."

INSIDE TIME WARNER AND ITS cable division, enthusiasm for FSN was starting to wane. What was the endgame? It had proven an appetite for VOD movies and interactive applications that could be potential money makers. It had helped to validate HFC architecture, client-server delivery, and MPEG video. But the network itself was expensive and challenging to run. Could it scale?

There was that buzz word: scale. A word that was new to cable endeavors because there was nothing like FSN before. A word that would put a dagger into the heart of FSN and many other digital projects to follow. A word that essentially meant *Can you grow this service and deploy it broadly without losing your shirt?*

"The one word that I didn't pay enough attention to, that really came to haunt me, was this notion of scalability. Was it scalable?" Levin said.

"It really became a learning lab," Carl Rossetti said. "We'd already proven the technology, and we weren't going to get anything more out of that. Plus, I think it stimulated the technology in terms of sending a message to the box guys to start working on what we see today. So it proved the market. You know, you could say, 'Well, it was a little bit ahead of its time,' but it did more than that. It stimulated this whole cable digital environment."

Meanwhile, other business strategies began occupying Levin's time. The media business was getting swept up in another wave of mergers and acquisitions. In the 1990s, M&A was a key strategy for many business sectors. It was favored by Wall Street and fueled by a variety of financial tools.

In September 1995, I was back in the same conference room where the FSN press announcement was made, this time watching Levin and a grinning Ted Turner as they agreed to merge Time Warner and Turner Broadcasting System in a $7.5-billion deal. The merger meant that CNN, TBS, TNT, and TCM were now under the Time Warner umbrella. Malone benefited too. TCI owned a stake in TBS, and Malone exacted favorable carriage rates for CNN and other Turner networks in exchange for his approval of the deal, according to Robichaux's *Cable Cowboy* book.

Turner was named vice chairman of Time Warner but soon found that his power was diluted. He frequently came into conflict with Levin and the Time Warner board and came to rue the day he made the merger deal. Things got worse for him during the AOL-Time Warner merger.

Time Warner Cable, meanwhile, grew into the largest cable operator in the country, expanding at a time when cable wasn't in vogue on Wall Street. In a series of deals, TWC acquired cable systems held by Paragon Cable and KBLCOM. It entered into a joint venture with Advance/Newhouse cable operations, started by the Newhouse media family and headed by Bob Miron. In 1996 it paid $2.6 billion for Cablevision Industries, built by Alan Gerry, who distributed nearly $100 million to many employees, according to the TWC history book *Making Connections*. Later, Gerry purchased the original site of the 1969 Woodstock music festival and transformed it into The Bethel Woods Center for the Arts, where Mike Egan, his former senior VP of programming, developed a museum telling the story of the 1960s and the Woodstock festival.

Wall Street began to recognize the potential for broadband cable, and Time Warner's stock soared, tripling in price over the span of several years before it split. Levin was credited for his commitment to cable, which became a lead engine for the company. But those accolades were later buried with the AOL Time Warner merger.

Though the future of FSN was coming into question, the company used it as a public affairs asset. Levin cited FSN during testimony before the Federal Trade Commission as it developed a consent decree on Time Warner's merger with Turner. "My own view is that this is a marvelous form—I don't mean to get philosophical about it—of self-actualization," Levin said, according to a *Cablevision* report.

During testimony before a House telecommunications subcommittee hearing about the 1996 Telecommunications Act, Levin cited FSN as a means for tailored consumer services, links between educational and medical institutions, and "the platform to offer to consumers, for the first time in a hundred years, a real choice in providers of local telephone service." Levin pointed to FSN as a service brought about through private enterprise, not public funding. Similarly, NCTA cited FSN in a campaign about advanced cable technology. It even highlighted the Willards.

The potential for interactive networks also raised a crucial question over whether they should be regulated as common carriers, as telephone carriers are. Privacy advocates raised concern about identifiable information, but for cable, there was a silver lining in the 1992 Cable Act, which restricted the use of customer information with third parties. Overall, policymakers left interactive TV alone, much as they did with the burgeoning internet.

CHAPTER 14
FLYING HORSE

Movies-on-demand proved to be the killer application that Time Warner was seeking (FSN Marketing Department. *Batman Returns*, a Warner Bros. film).

EVEN AT THE TIME OF FSN's launch, many of the engineers recognized that FSN could not be deployed widely with the costly, cumbersome early-generation equipment that was being used. After the December 1994 launch, TWC's advanced engineering team returned to its Denver headquarters and quietly began drawing plans for "the deployable FSN." The idea was to generate affordable digital set-top boxes—not ones that cost $4,500 each—and provide customers with hundreds of digital channels and on-demand options.

The project was named Pegasus, after the mythical flying horse. It eventually took root two years later when TWC issued an RFP (request for proposals) for 1 million digital set-tops.

TWC also began developing its high-speed internet access service, code named Excalibur and eventually branded as Road Runner. Before they could launch it, they had to pay Warner Bros. a handsome sum for use of its trademarked Road Runner cartoon character, according to sources. Engineers recognized that the same infrastructure that was being put into place in Orlando could also support internet access, provided that requisite modems and transmission equipment materialized. Later, FSN was erroneously credited for launching high-speed internet, but TWC's first market test was reported to be in 1995 in Elmira, NY.

Glenn Britt said it was a logical step to transition from FSN to internet access because FSN really "was a computer network. The only thing different between it and Road Runner was that the display was a television rather than a PC monitor. Because of the point in time, there was not standard software. Today there are all these standards around the internet."

Industry debates raged over whether interactive TV or the internet would win out. News coverage reflected the difference in perspective over those two mediums. *The Tampa Business Journal* ran a story headed: "Time Warner: Interactive TV still relevant," quoting company officials saying the company planned to offer internet access to complement the FSN, not supplant it. The exact same story appeared in a sister publication, *The Orlando Business Journal*, with a very different spin: "Interactive television generates yawns now that 'everybody has web mania.'"

Despite initial progress, competing projects faced challenges. In 1996 Bell Atlantic said its VOD Stargazer trial for about 1,000 homes in Northern Virginia achieved buy rates that were twelve times higher than PPV. Stargazer featured a flashy interface that opened with a silver orb flying through a community and then presented a page with options for entertainment, learning and lifestyles, kids' zone, and "reel values."

But the ability to provide video over copper phone lines was limited. Bell Atlantic, along with Ameritech and NYNEX, backed off plans for video dial tone service by telling the FCC it was "technologically outmoded," according to *Washington Technology*. Regulatory issues were likely a bigger barrier. Richard Notebaert, chairman and CEO of Ameritech, told the publication that the FCC wanted to regulate VDT services as if they were common carrier telephone lines, subjecting them to potential rate regulation. Municipalities would likely require local cable franchise regulations. "The two sets of rules make it impossible to operate," he said.

US West shut down an interactive shopping service called US Avenue and an information service, GoTV, though FSN kept GoTV running. Meanwhile, Cox Communications ended an interactive trial in Omaha, NE. Alex Best, senior VP of engineering for Cox Communications at the time, heralded FSN's accomplishments but said, for Cox, "it was obvious the technology was not ready for prime time."

The Sega Channel, cable's potential entrée into the video-game market, ran into difficulties with its cable-based service. The service downloaded 16-bit games to a Genesis game player for a monthly subscription fee. It was being outpaced by 32-bit consoles, including Sega's own Saturn console. On the horizon were 64-bit processors that provided better memory for gaming performance, including Nintendo 64, developed in partnership with SGI.

"Like so many young digital ventures, Sega showed great promise but couldn't move past the nascent tech and operational limitations of its time," said Mark Hess, who'd moved from TCI to handle Sega affiliate relations. The business model wasn't working either. Hess explained, "Fifty games per month for one low price sounds great to a ten-year-old. Not so good to a mother."

After Sega, Hess joined Comcast and was instrumental in its digital product rollouts. Sega Channel's head of sales and marketing, Clayton Banks, became a leader in interactive media and the cofounder and

CEO of Silicon Harlem, dedicated to bringing advanced technologies to Upper Manhattan and other urban areas.

The ITV naysayers grew. "The interactive TV industry has gone into a stall," a Forrester Research analyst said. "People are losing sleep committing millions and ultimately billions to trials and rollouts." A financial analyst was quoted as saying that an FSN rollout to other TWC system wasn't going to happen because "I think they've already had that inflated optimism knocked out of them some time ago." The WebTV concept began generating a resurgence in talk of industry convergence, that perhaps the best strategy was just to slap the internet onto TV sets.

The consumer proposition behind ITV was getting questioned. *Wired* correspondent Evan Schwartz traveled around the country to see ITV services in demos or live homes where possible. He observed GTE's mainStreet near Boston, Microsoft's prototype in Redmond, FSN in Orlando, and Bell Atlantic's Virginia trial.

"All these corporations have the same top-down view of how they can force a change in people's entrenched viewing habits. They all project how revenue will shift from other industries, such as retailing, into their own," Schwartz wrote. "I'll just stay the spud I am. I just want to plop down on the sofa, turn on the entertainment, tune out my higher brain functions, and exercise my constitutional right to stare vacantly at the tube, resting assured that interactive television is still little more than an oxymoron."

More companies turned their attention toward the viability of internet access over cable infrastructure. Viacom Cable, led by John Goddard, began some of the first installations of cable modems. In Castro Valley, CA, where it had been experimenting with ITV, Viacom tested modems supplied by General Instrument and Intel. Among the Viacom engineers was Doug Semon, who later joined TWC and married Leslie Ellis.

TCI, with affiliate InterMedia Partners, headed by Leo Hindery, bought Viacom's cable systems in 1995 for $2.3 billion during an ongoing dispute between Malone and Redstone over carriage fees for Viacom's networks. Malone named Hindery president of TCI in 1997. Viacom, no longer a cable system owner, focused on its content-is-king strategy.

TWC launched Road Runner commercially in 1996, claiming it as the first cable-delivered high-speed internet access service. The FSN experience was helpful in rolling out Road Runner, said Rossetti, who served as the unit's interim CEO. He explained, "By the time we got to Road Runner, we knew certain things. We understood how to manage it. We understood how to market it better. There was a little blueprint from the Full Service Network."

Meanwhile, the telcos continued their relentless pursuit to get into television and provide VOD and interactive services, even though video dial tone was no longer tenable. Based upon Bell Atlantic's development of Stargazer, telcos Pacific Telesis and NYNEX joined the company in Tele-TV, a venture promising to offer VOD and interactive shopping. Creative Artists Agency, headed by legendary Hollywood agent Michael Ovitz, was part of the venture. To move the telcos into the TV world, Tele-TV hired Howard Stringer, president of the CBS Broadcast Group, as CEO and former Fox executive Sandy Grushow as president, according to a Wikipedia history.

A second joint venture, Americast, formed to move other telcos into the TV business. It included Southwestern Bell Company (SBC), BellSouth, Ameritech, GTE, and Southern New England Telecommunications. Americast selected Disney's Televenture subsidiary as a programming partner, and it ordered $1-billion worth of digital set-top boxes from Zenith Electronics, according to the *Los Angeles Times*.

By 1996, nearly every major telco in America, banded together in two joint ventures, was taking aim at cable's business. On February 8, 1996, President Clinton signed the 1996 Telecommunications

Act into law, allowing the phone companies to move into cable. Less than three weeks later, US West announced it was purchasing Continental Cablevision, the company founded by Amos Hostetter. The telco paid $5.3 billion in cash and stock and assumed $5.6 billion in debt, according to an online history, *The Continental Cablevision Story*, spearheaded by former Continental executive and NCTA president Robert Sachs.

The US West-Continental relationship was another case of oil and water. According to the online history, US West reneged on a promise to keep the Continental management team intact and in Boston, leading Hostetter and several of his top executives to resign. The cable operation, renamed MediaOne, ultimately faltered and was sold to AT&T Broadband in 1999, which Comcast bought in 2002.

Not long after the Telecommunications Act took effect, the former Bell companies began to reassemble into two new phone giants. Bell Atlantic and NYNEX merged and then purchased GTE to form Verizon, which launched its fiber-based Fios TV service in 2005. SBC led the charge to acquire the other Baby Bells in a newly formed AT&T, which launched its U-verse TV service in 2006. With Fios and U-verse, the cable industry had a new two-headed monster to contend with.

■ ▶ ▶▶

LUDINGTON LEFT FSN AT THE end of 1996. Having mashed together technologies through brute force integration, he recognized that technology integration was going to be a key need in the industry. He launched his own business, called INT2 for Internetwork Integration, to help cable and tech companies sort through the integration challenges and push the boundaries of HFC architecture.

FSN had given Ludington everything an enterprising engineer could want. It was a giant sandbox where he could build sandcastles that reached into the sky. He broke free from his analog roots and branched out into digital and broadband. He got an inside look at what digital video and interactive media could provide. He made friends and had a lot of laughs. He parted FSN with a rousing going-away party. As a parting gift, the entire staff signed one of his favorite FSN promo posters. But it was by no means the last time he would play a key role with TWC.

There was a more important thing he gained at FSN: a spouse. Colleen, his wife, worked in Time Warner's interactive shopping group with Time Warner programming executive Thayer Bigelow. She got stationed at FSN, where she supported shopping order fulfillment. Ludington first met her during a Cable Show in New Orleans. He saw her on Bourbon Street by The Famous Door music club and thought, *I've got to meet that girl.* He did, and the rest is Ludington family history.

■ ▶ ▶▶

Time Warner sought to position Pegasus as a transitional step from FSN, preparing for the projects' inevitable fate. In December 1996, TWC announced its selection of S-A as prime contractor for Pegasus, with Pioneer, Toshiba, and General Instrument as set-top providers. Chiddix said in the press release, "Our experience with the Full Service Network has demonstrated the strong potential of true video-on-demand."

The press didn't accept the PR spin. On April 2, 1997, came one of the most negative pieces about the project. *The Los Angeles Times* ran a 1,400-word piece headed: "Time Warner's Interactive TV Project Blinks." The story said, "With a string of missed deadlines, red ink, and failure to deliver promised goods such as residential phone service over its cable lines, experts say Time Warner's ambitious project has become a costly dinosaur that is rapidly being overtaken by a simpler but vastly more popular interactive network: the internet. Time Warner executives have already largely consigned some FSN services, such as home shopping, to the internet because the global network is better suited to transactional business."

The story also noted, "Vice President Al Gore, who has been a leading proponent of interactive cable networks, recently rebuked the industry for not moving swiftly enough. 'I'm a little surprised that the cable industry has not gone further than it has' to modernize its networks for high-speed interactive communications, Gore said in a recent interview with reporters."

While FSN's star was fading, Time Warner's was rising. The company posted strong first-quarter 1997 financial results. *Multichannel News* reported, "While Tele-Communications Inc. has panicked cable investors by jamming through harsh rate hikes but failing to increase cash flow, Time Warner is pulling it off... 'These are great numbers,' said Bear Stearns media analyst Ray Katz. 'A lot of it has to do with Orlando,' said another analyst, who noted that Time Warner has stopped heavy spending on its over-hyped Full Service Network operation there."

On April 23, 1997, TWC started backing away from FSN and pointing to Pegasus as the shiny new thing. A press release heralded the Pegasus digital box program "to support full Video On Demand and Road Runner to the television." Hayashi was quoted: "Without the knowledge gained from the Full Service Network, this would not have been possible."

Only a week later, on April 30, the company issued the follow-up press release:

> Full Service Network to Wind Down in Orlando by Year End; Time Warner Cable Prepares For Pegasus Video On Demand Rollout
>
> Time Warner Cable announced today that as the video on demand development process for its Pegasus digital system intensifies during 1997, The Full Service Network office in Orlando will wind down its current activities and is expected to close by the end of the year.

"The Full Service Network has demonstrated with great success that video on demand is a powerful business we believe can be deployed in the near future, based on strong customer demand and the decreasing cost of delivering video to the home," said Glenn Britt, president of Time Warner Cable Ventures. "The value of the Orlando experiment to Time Warner has been tremendous. In addition to providing the technical and marketing data that made possible our Pegasus program, the FSN's early results provided the foundation for our Road Runner service, which is now launched in four markets, with many more to come . . .

"The Full Service Network team is proud of the role it has played in pioneering video on demand and gratified it is now moving toward commercial deployment," said FSN President Tom Feige. "We successfully overcame incredible challenges in becoming the first to converge technologies from the cable, computer, and telephone industries to stream full motion video on demand to customers' homes. Along with our technical achievements, we successfully introduced digital services that customers not only are willing to pay for but also find fun and easy to use."

USA Today reported, "Time Warner Cancels Full Service Network: Entertainment giant Time Warner made it official Wednesday. It is closing the Full Service Network, its much-hyped interactive TV operation in Orlando, FL. . . . FSN never fulfilled the dreams of its champion, Time Warner CEO Gerald Levin. He predicted in 1994 that the Orlando system would become a prototype for cable and 'a turning point for the communications industry.'"

"Once Heralded, Quietly Abandoned Interactive TV Idea Fades As Orlando Test Ends," said *The Philadelphia Inquirer*. "The tombstone for the project was all but hidden in a news release devoted to Time

Warner's future plans. Yet it serves as a quiet, almost whispered coda to several years of electrifying noise and buzz and frenzy about a futuristic, 500-channel world that was supposed to be just around the corner."

"High Hopes Drowned in Dollars," said *America's Network*, a telecommunications magazine that met its own demise. "All new network trials share at least one thing: hype. However, when the headlines diminish and media attention goes elsewhere, only the network successes will remain in the spotlight. FSN will not have that pleasure." The project "was essentially a failure and has become the most notable casualty on the road to the digital Interactive Age."

Chiddix, in a Cable Center interview in 2000, said, "The press turned ugly and has ever since called it Time Warner's failed interactive trial in Orlando. Well, in fact it didn't fail, and there were a number of trials that did fail. A number of companies announced these things and were unable to make them work. We made this work, we got it to real customers, they spent real money on it, and we explored a new business, and along the way we stumbled around the edges of what became the web."

Coverage of the phaseout announcement was not as heavy as either the delay announcement or the launch reports. Ed Adler surmised that the announcement was "anticlimactic, and people in the media knew it was coming."

Customers were disappointed by the shutdown. The *Orlando Sentinel* reported, "News of the shutdown caught customers and vendors by surprise . . . Susan and Karl Willard of Longwood, who played video games with Time Warner Chief Executive Gerald Levin when the system debuted, said they will miss it. 'They still had some bugs in it, but it's a good system,' Susan Willard said."

With the shutdown of The News Exchange, *Sentinel* Editor John Haile praised FSN as a technological marvel and valuable learning tool for the newspaper. A Barnett Bank spokesperson said FSN customers used the at-home banking app at a rate nearly three times that of the bank's online site. "Customers very much liked this channel," she said.

Some trade press reporters took a somewhat kinder tone. *Multimedia Monitor*, a newsletter, said "Time-Warner's ITV Test Fails—But Not Totally: Although Time Warner Cable is shutting down its vaunted and costly Full Service Network interactive television service in Orlando, Fla.—a move that had been expected for some time—it cannot be denied that the test project served a useful purpose to highlight what works in interactive television models and what doesn't."

FSN employees, reportedly numbering 158 at the time, were said to be disappointed by the shutdown, although for many it wasn't unexpected. In my discussions, employees were universally proud of their experience. But several harbored some bitterness over the outcome and questioned whether Time Warner was being shortsighted by training a team in interactive technology and then letting them go. FSN workers suffered a familiar outcome of many ITV projects: unemployment.

That spring, Levin publicly addressed the shifting fortunes of interactive TV in remarks at a technology conference. According to a press account, he said, "Three years ago, I ventured a series of predictions. . . . At their center was the notion that digital interactivity would arrive faster than anyone thought and that its momentum would arise not out of consumer interest in the elegant symmetry of its electronic architecture but because of the access it gives to a wide variety of services and programming choices."

Levin said he was "on the money" about the message. "Interactivity has become an important presence in the media mix with amazing suddenness," he said. "Whether by themselves or through partnerships, those who dismissed it as a pipe dream are scrambling to become part of the pipe." But Levin said he was "off the mark—at least in the short run—about the medium. Before long, all the media—PC, TV, DVD—will be driven by the same digital brain. But for the moment, interactive TV continues to be largely experimental, while the internet has taken off."

Standard protocols, open architecture, and scalability—that's what made the internet take off. Not proprietary schemes and limited distribution platforms. But the internet and ITV shared one thing: the constant race by moguls and companies to control the medium and own the consumer. Soon, Levin was back with a grander plan.

THE PROJECT WAS CHRISTENED WITH the label of "the failed FSN." Memories quickly became skewed over what it was and sometimes contained errors. A *New York Times* story in October 1998 said, "Previous attempts to provide video-on-demand, like Time Warner's 500-channel cable system in Orlando, have failed." A book released in the fall of 1998, titled *The Billionaire Shell Game: How Cable Baron John Malone and Assorted Corporate Titans Invented a Future Nobody Wanted*, by L.J. Davis, ridiculed cable's interactive efforts and said the only thing that anyone learned about FSN was that people like to buy stamps. The book skewered Malone for conjuring up the supposedly fanciful notion of a 500-channel universe, even though everything Malone predicted with digital compression was coming true—and then some.

Joe Collins said, "If you think back, there was this great expectation given that the announcement that we made initially happened at the same time a lot of other people were talking about things that they were doing. Bell Atlantic, about what they were going to do somewhere in New Jersey. US West was going to do something in Omaha. TCI was talking about 500 channels. So, right off the bat, there was a great expectation created, not just about us in this particular project but about all these things that were generally coming. And it made it seem as though it was coming a lot faster than it was. It created a belief that this wasn't a grand designers' test, but this was real, the seed of the tree, and it was going to grow right out of the seed into the whole plant. I can't think of how we could have swum too successfully against the tide, because the tide was running pretty strong."

Fred Dressler, TWC's senior VP of programming, blamed hype about the project for creating the impression that it was a failure. "It was hardly a failed experiment, because everything that we're doing today is really built off the back of what we learned there. And what we learned was that people loved on-demand, the ability to choose the programming that they wanted," Dressler said in a 2005 interview for The Cable Center. "It was an enormous success if you want to look at it from the fact that it was necessary to do in order to get to where we are today. It was a failure if you thought everything we did then was going to work."

It certainly didn't help that Levin started off by saying FSN wasn't a trial. But he stood by the project through thick and thin. "I think it was his way of nailing himself to the mast on this and challenging everyone not to let him down. I think it was a classic example of CEO leadership, even to the point where he was putting himself on the line more than we were comfortable with," Luftman said.

The big guessing game was this: What did FSN cost? A couple stories about the shutdown cited an unnamed source saying the estimated cost was about $200 to 300 million. *Multichannel News* and other publications took to calling it the "$300-million FSN," practically daring Time Warner to confirm or deny the figure. The company remained mum. Based upon some analysis of the cost of the servers, HCTs, and overhead, the estimate seemed plausible. That estimate, however, did not take into account the incalculable cost to many Time Warner divisions and partner companies for their manpower, as well as the time and effort to support the project.

Was it worth it? Had FSN been presented as an R&D project, perhaps the verdicts wouldn't have been so harsh. It might be a bit self-serving, but those involved argued that the cost was well worth it.

"FSN had so many influences on the industry," said Kanouff, who went on to become a leader in VOD and interactive media. "We learned so much about VOD management, which turned out to be the VOD standards of the industry. Network infrastructure and modulation techniques are still implemented today. Not only on the technology side, but user interfaces and interactive TV behavior was all innovated with the FSN."

Allen Ecker, one of the leading brains behind Scientific Atlanta's development of digital technology, cited "a lot of firsts" that sustained the industry for years. Engineers gained insights into using HFC architecture and QAM for digital. FSN gave engineers valuable experience with handling reverse paths, overcoming corrupted signals with such techniques as forward-error correction, and syncing digital video and audio, he said.

While the project was expensive, TWC learned things that saved the company money in the long run, according to the engineers. The big, expensive ATM switch produced a syncing issue with video and audio so characters appeared to be dubbed in a foreign movie. Largely through the design work of Michael Adams, they learned to remove ATM switches, which Chiddix noted was a potential multimillion-dollar savings.

In conferences and other forums, Mike LaJoie, who became chief technology officer for Time Warner Cable, repeatedly said FSN was worth whatever the cost. If it had been presented as an R&D project from the beginning, the cost would have been easily justified by onlookers, he said. In a *Multichannel News* column marking FSN's tenth launch anniversary, LaJoie said, "As the FSN wound down in 1997, we were chastised by some for engaging in what was obviously an expensive initiative. We think it was worth it. Given the array of advances it helped birth, there are those today who look at the FSN investment as a relative bargain."

CHAPTER 15
REQUIEM

Prometheus in gilded cast bronze in Rockefeller Center (Paul Manship, *Prometheus* statue, 1934; photo from Wikimedia Commons).

IN THE HEART OF MANHATTAN, as mortals went about the business of plotting to dominate each other using new digital weaponry, the mighty bronze Prometheus stood in Rockefeller Center, his left hand still reached toward the stainless-steel relief of artist Isamu Noguchi's ode to journalists of a bygone era. The revolving doors to the Time Warner building still spun. Prometheus is clearly portrayed as a hero. The etching in the wall behind him proclaims that he is a teacher in every art who brought fire to mortals.

But the Greek gods knew better. For Prometheus *stole* the fire that he gave to man. And for that, Zeus sentenced him to eternal torture.

■ ▶ ▶▶

Jerry Levin's son Jonathan eschewed the trappings of a rich and privileged life. Rather than use his father's wealth to sail the world or be a wine taster (as he predicted he would be in his high school yearbook), he became an English teacher at William H. Taft High School in the Bronx. Jonathan loved the Yankees and rap music and was a dedicated teacher, taking extra time to support the school's attempts to prevent students from dropping out, according to an in-depth *Newsweek* account by Alexander Nazaryan.

In early June 1997, about the same time as FSN was shutting down, Jerry Levin received the horrible news. Jonathan was found dead in his apartment. He had stab wounds, and he'd been fatally shot. Soon, the police zeroed in on a prime suspect: one of Jonathan's own students. The student and an accomplice tortured and killed Jonathan in a botched robbery attempt in which they sought to use Jonathan's ATM bank code to steal his father's fortune. They got away with the maximum withdrawal amount: $800. The student, Corey Arthur, was eventually convicted of murder, while the accomplice, who signed a confession implicating Arthur, was acquitted. (Nazaryan's article in 2016 raised questions about whether Arthur truly was the trigger man and whether his twenty-five-to-life prison sentence fit his role in the crime.)

How could anything be worse? During the exhausting trial of his son's murderer the following year, Jerry and Jonathan's mother, Carol, were forced to endure the grim details that reverberated in sensational tabloid headlines day after day.

Under this dark cloud, I was scheduled to interview Levin as part of a follow-up on FSN. On a cool October morning, I arrived at the Time Warner building at 75 Rockefeller Center. The timing of the interview was terrible. The murder trial was still ongoing. That morning, *The New York Times* reported that defense lawyers had argued that an episode of the TV series *NYPD Blue* closely resembled the Levin case and that any juror who saw it would be unable to decide the case fairly. The judge disagreed (also the TV producers denied they were replicating the Levin case), but it conjured concern that justice in the case might not be served.

I went through the Time Warner golden revolving doors, and Ed Adler escorted me to a small conference room, where I sat at an ornate wooden table. We waited for Levin for what seemed like an eternity, my stomach churning all the while. I didn't like anything about the situation and suggested that we could reschedule the interview.

Then the door opened, and in walked Levin. His face was ashen, and the weight of the world was upon him.

He sat down at the table, staring at the polished wood. "What is this about?" he asked. I explained that I wanted to ask him about the FSN project. But I offered to do the interview another time.

"Give me a minute," he said, still staring at the table. And then the light shone in his eyes, and he began to speak. He talked about the genesis of the project, the early meetings, the opportunities for digital services, and what the company learned. He provided a cogent history, with sharp recollections. I had a legal pad with about twenty questions to ask him, but I think I asked about three. He seemed to know where to go next and continued down my list of questions without me even asking.

His eyes lit up thinking about the culture of innovation in Orlando. "Here, we'd have these prosaic problems back in the home office, but, boy, when you talked to somebody in Orlando or went down there, it was the most exhilarating experience. I mean, it was like I'd get a fix to go down there, and they'd give me a remote control so I could play with the system."

Ultimately, did he take responsibility for the expense of a project that couldn't scale? Most assuredly. He said he'd kept hearing about the promise of switched networks, Moore's law, and cheaper servers and set-tops. "So I actually believed that this was not a test or an experiment, but it was the launch of a service," he said. "I think, you know, maybe our egos overtook us a little bit. But I think that's a terrific development in the history of the business."

Levin seemed indifferent to FSN being called a failure. He noted that all of the major cable, telecom, and computer companies have embraced digital broadband and many of the technologies pioneered by FSN.

"Whether you get the recognition or not probably doesn't matter," Levin said. Though he added, "It should matter to all the people who worked really hard on this. They really created something that was amazing and don't get enough credit for it. And isn't that true of most advances, that you have to do these things before they're apparent? If you do it when it's apparent and it's easy to do, then everybody does it."

Under the circumstances, the interview with Levin was the most extraordinary interview in my career. When we were done, we got up to leave, and Levin walked toward the door. Before departing, he turned to me and said one last thing: "You know, I have a tape of the FSN launch event. Every time I watch it, I get tears in my eyes."

DESPITE THE DEMISE OF FSN, the quest for the Holy Grail of ITV continued across the industry. Cable providers sought to add interactive program guides (IPGs) that could serve as platforms for user-friendly TV navigation, on-demand content, and interactive features. Dozens of wealthy media players, experienced companies, and aspiring start-ups sought to provide a platform, device, or software to enable ITV. Madison Avenue continued to explore ways that TV commercials could include interactive elements or instant purchases through t-commerce.

Gates and Microsoft continued to seek their stake in the TV game and become the central facilitator of what became known as "the connected home." TCI and Microsoft prepared for an ITV trial for 2,000 homes in Redmond, WA, to test Microsoft's OS, media server, and FSN-like services, including an interactive guide, movies-on-demand, games, and information services.

Microsoft spread its wings by building partnerships with telcos, system integrators, and OEMs (original equipment manufacturers). It put its moniker on TV by joining NBC to be the MS in the MSNBC cable network that launched in 1996. It developed products across the spectrum of TV delivery and developed platforms for IPTV (internet protocol TV, essentially streaming of TV channels).

But Microsoft's many propositions to partner with US cable providers were like a forlorn suitor wooing with flowers and candy but largely getting ignored. In June 1997, the company invested $1 billion in Comcast, a stake it held until 2009. In 1998, Gates, having shown he was willing to buy his way in, made a personal appeal to partner with the cable industry in a keynote speech at NCTA's The Cable Show.

Road Runner provided another opportunity for Gates to show up with flowers. Microsoft and computer company Compaq invested a combined $425 million in a Road Runner joint venture that at that point included Time Warner, Advance/Newhouse, and MediaOne. The plan called for Compaq to produce and ship cable-ready PCs and Microsoft to provide its experience in internet, client-server, and application software, according to CNET. The investment gave Microsoft and Compaq, later purchased by Hewlett-Packard, each a 10 percent stake in the venture.

Looking back at all the investments, joint ventures, and consortiums in the early days of digital, it's hard to determine whether companies were following sound strategies or making haphazard bets. The strategy seemed to amount to little more than this: Plant a few hundred million here and there, and see if something grows.

Although it was unable to deliver a sub-$300 set-top for TCI, Microsoft provided a middleware platform for an advanced Motorola set-top box, the DCT-5000. The box was to be the ultimate TV device, including both Microsoft and Java middleware and a modem for all manner of interactive apps. It was expensive for cable operators, and it experienced software glitches, according to *Multichannel News*. Models were delivered to Comcast but didn't make it out of the warehouse, sources said. By 2002, the much-anticipated DCT-5000 was retired. Karen Brown wrote, "They didn't even give it a gold retirement watch."

Digital set-tops still represented a hefty expense for cable operators. Their capital budgets were already strained by upgrading and rebuilding cable systems to increase their bandwidth for digital channels and high-speed internet. Operators could amortize the cost of an existing set-top and charge a monthly lease fee for it, so there wasn't a big financial incentive to switch out boxes. Although Moore's law was chugging along, to add enough memory and processing to support an IPG, HDTV and interactivity would significantly boost the price of digital set-tops.

Mark Hess, the former Comcast executive, said, "That was the biggest problem: getting enough memory and processing into these devices early on. It was just too expensive."

Gate's former partner, Microsoft cofounder Paul Allen, purchased Charter Communications in a $4.5-billion deal in 1998, creating the fourth largest US cable company at the time. Espousing a "wired world" strategy, Allen, then the third richest person in the US, and his Vulcan Ventures investment arm made many deals to marry connectivity and entertainment. According to a profile in *The Guardian*, the investments included stakes in Barry Diller's USA Networks; $100 million in Oxygen Media, a women's cable channel founded by Gerry Laybourne; and a $500-million investment in Hollywood studio DreamWorks.

Allen continued his cable shopping spree by spending nearly $2.8 billion to buy Marcus Cable, founded by Jeff Marcus and headed by Lou Borrelli, who eventually became CEO of the National Content & Technology Cooperative, representing small cable and broadband providers. In 1999, Allen paid $3.1 billion to add Bresnan

Communications to its cable system properties. That company was headed by another early cable pioneer, Bill Bresnan, who was instrumental in founding The Cable Center. Later Bresnan reentered the business by acquiring former AT&T Broadband cable systems in Western states that were eventually purchased by Cablevision Systems.

Allen also launched an ITV company, Digeo, which offered a Moxi Media Center set-top box and an on-screen portal for interactive content that looked similar to streaming service home pages today. More impressive was the yacht on which Allen invited cable executives and reporters to promote Digeo, featuring a sound studio where Allen played with famous musicians, a helicopter, and a submarine.

In 1999, Microsoft announced it would invest $5 billion in AT&T Corp. The companies said they would use Microsoft software in its set-top boxes and establish an open platform for ITV apps, according to CNET. Later, AT&T utilized Microsoft's Mediaroom IPTV platform to launch U-verse, a triple-play offering of pay TV, internet, and phone service. While AT&T claimed the service was fiber-based, the *HuffPost* found that in most areas, it was delivered over traditional copper phone lines. That may have dispelled AT&T's claim, but it didn't diminish that delivering the IPTV service over copper was a significant technological feat.

Another major computer industry player, Larry Ellison's Oracle Corp., spawned Liberate Technologies (a.k.a. Liberate TV), offering server software and middleware for interactive TV services. Gary Lauder, a bright and engaging scion of the Estee Lauder family fortune, created ActiveVideo (nee ICTV), offering a CloudTV platform for weblike pages of cable networks and other fare. From France came ITV software provider Canal Plus Technologies, whose US marketer Arthur Orduna would go on to become chief technology and products officer of Canoe Ventures, a cable-backed enterprise that initially attempted to establish a t-commerce platform.

Sony's ITV aspirations increased in 1999 when it struck a deal, valued at more than $1 billion, to deploy an ITV service for Chuck and Jim Dolan's Cablevision Systems in New York. The service "will let viewers watch video-on-demand, search the internet, use email, and play video games through a set-top box built by Sony," *Variety* reported. Sony said it had a commitment for 3 million set-tops, designed to use a wireless keyboard for interactive activity. Howard Stringer, who followed Tele-TV by becoming chairman and CEO of Sony Corp. of America, said Cablevision would be "the industry leader in the biggest market in America with the richest customers." Over the ensuing years, Cablevision offered games, shopping, and enhanced content, including an interactive Barbie channel that could be managed with a TV remote. But eventually, the apps were discontinued.

Simultaneously, the cable industry sought to stake its claim in internet services. TCI, Comcast, and Cox Communications joined founders Milo Medin and William Randolph Hearst III, of the Hearst media family, in @Home Network, a cable high-speed internet service that would provide connectivity plus a portal to content and applications. To fulfill the latter mission, in 1999, @Home Network acquired internet portal Excite in a $6.7-billion merger. Many other cable providers joined to offer co-branded @Home services, except for Time Warner Cable. It was focused on Road Runner and a potential portal plan, although the parent corporation's Pathfinder portal with Time Inc. publications was a financial disaster that was shut down in 1999. Ultimately, @Home was another case of a service getting thwarted by tough economics and bad timing. It got swept away in the dot-com crash, its stock price plummeted, and it filed for bankruptcy protection in 2001.

But before @Home met its demise, Malone and Leo Hindery, TCI's president and CEO, used it to help attract AT&T CEO Mike Armstrong to buy TCI in 1998 in a $48-billion all-stock deal. It's widely acknowledged that AT&T vastly overpaid for TCI. AT&T also purchased MediaOne, the former Continental Cablevision systems, for $57 billion, just four years after the company had been valued at five times less. The stock-heavy deals looked even worse when

AT&T's share price fell by more than one-half. AT&T's dalliance with cable system ownership only lasted until 2002, when the renamed AT&T Broadband was sold to Comcast in a deal valued at $72 billion, vaulting Comcast to the top ranking of cable and broadband companies, serving more than 22 million subscribers.

Throughout the late '90s, the cable industry put the pieces in place for its digital transition. The requirements that seemed unfathomable at the 1992 Western Show were gradually moving into the field. Companies were laying more fiber and installing the first digital set-tops. In 1998, the cable industry collectively invested nearly $8 billion for infrastructure improvements, primarily to accommodate two-way services, including high-speed internet and phone, according to The Cable Center's records.

Outside of Denver, TCI established a large satellite uplink facility called Headend in the Sky (HITS) to feed more channels to cable systems. Time Warner built a similar satellite-delivery system, Athena. To fuel VOD, a crop of companies arose offering servers and other support, including Concurrent, DIVA, Intertainer, nCUBE, SeaChange, and TVN Entertainment Corp. (now Vubiquity).

Meanwhile, television was undergoing another milestone advancement: high-definition. After years of wrangling among broadcasters, consumer electronics manufacturers, and other involved parties in a so-called Grand Alliance, Advanced Television Systems Committee (ATSC) digital broadcast standards were adopted. The rocky road to HDTV is chronicled in Joel Brinkley's book, *Defining Vision: How Broadcasters Lured the Government into Inciting a Revolution in Television*.

HDTV sets moved into the marketplace in 1998 and marked one of the most far-reaching developments in TV history. HDTV required an expensive retrofitting of virtually every part of television technology: transmitters, studios, cameras, production equipment, everything. Broadcast and cable networks had to choose between two primary transmission standards: 1080i interlaced scan or 720p progressive scan. Newscasters and TV personalities had to find the right facial makeup to look good in the unfiltered clarity of high definition. HD attracted another billionaire to the TV game: Mark Cuban was a founding partner in HDNet, an all-HD channel later rebranded as AXS TV.

HDTV transformed American living rooms (and furniture) with new flat-screen TVs, providing crystal-clear pictures and sound. Consumers had to decipher the difference between models, including plasma TV, LCD (liquid crystal display), or LED (light emitting diode). Initial HDTV sets cost $8,000, according to *The New York Times*, but by 2010 many models (before smart TVs and 4K ultra-HD models were available) were priced at less than $600. Based upon annual sales estimates by the Consumer Technology Association (née Consumer Electronics Association), from 1998 through 2010, Americans spent approximately $100 billion on HDTV sets.

HD had consequences for cable's 500-channel universe too. A single HD channel consumed about three to four channels worth of digital bandwidth. For a time, cable systems had to carry analog, standard definition (SD), and HD signals, often simulcasting three versions of the same channel. In sum, the abundant space provided by digital compression got eaten by the HD bandwidth hog. By comparison, launching an initial internet service could be accomplished by using only one to two digital channels worth of bandwidth. So cable operators could start two new product lines—internet service and voice-over internet phone—by using about the same amount of bandwidth as a couple of HD channels. And there were no license fees to pay to programmers.

As the twenty-first century arrived, the prospects for exciting new digital services seemed bright. But for the companies providing them, there was more unexpected disruption to come.

CHAPTER 16
THE OFFSPRING

TiVo's cofounder said inventing the first digital video recorder was a "natural extension" of FSN (logo by TiVo 2011 from Wikimedia Commons).

SHORTLY AFTER **FSN** SHUT DOWN, two members of SGI's Orlando team, Jim Barton and Mike Ramsay, met for lunch in Los Gatos, CA. They were itching to do something new in the digital realm. Silicon Valley was swimming in venture capital money for start-ups. Most of the investors' focus was on the wellspring of imaginative ideas for the internet. FSN had scratched the surface of what could be done with television.

Ramsay, in a retrospective for online forum *Medium*, said, "We talked about how it would be great if your home had a capability to manage all of your media. A home server idea. It was a natural extension of what happened in the Orlando project."

At SGI, Barton worked with Jim Clark and a small team that proposed the development of a new kind of television set-top with 3D graphics capability and support for new applications, including VOD, according to Barton's bio. He became VP and general manager of a Media Systems division formed to productize headend and server technology for ITV systems, based upon developments at FSN. The division was folded into Interactive Digital Solutions, a joint venture between SGI and AT&T Network Systems that supported ITV rollouts for service providers, including Chuck Dolan's Cablevision Systems on Long Island. Ramsay served as a senior VP of SGI's Silicon Desktop Group, working on the company's graphically rich workstations.

Eventually, Barton and Ramsay came upon a perfect marriage of software and hardware. If television programming was routed through a hard drive, it could be recorded and managed like a VCR, but it wouldn't require any clunky videocassette tapes or discs. There was an additional, amazing feature. Live programming—actual real-time action—could be paused and then played on a viewer's own time. This was a mind-blowing concept. How could something that's happening now be frozen in time? To put the concept into practice, the duo launched a start-up called Teleworld, later renamed TiVo.

Ramsay served as chairman and CEO and Barton as CTO. In 1999 their team introduced the first TiVo DVR, which some called a personal video recorder or PVR. Taking convenience to a new level, the TiVo box included a hard drive that enabled viewers to magically record, pause, and replay live TV. And if you could pause and then Fast Forward through the live programming, that meant you could skip right through the commercials. Bye-bye McDonald's, Budweiser, and Chevrolet.

Upon setting up my first TiVo and showing it to my then five-year-old daughter Kate, she happily told me, "Now I'll never have to watch ads." From out of the mouths of babes.

The DVR terrified TV networks and Madison Avenue, fearing that it meant the end of commercial TV. A Sunday *New York Times Magazine* article, by Michael Lewis in August 2000, declared the demise of TV commercials due to TiVo. The article was accompanied by photos of burned-out TV sets and exploding cereal boxes.

While DVRs didn't cause cereal boxes to explode, they spurred the industry to take action. By 2007, Nielsen introduced C3 ratings, a measure of the commercials watched both live and up to three days later through DVR playback. At least with TiVo, viewers had to Fast Forward through the ads so they would catch a glimpse. A competitor, ReplayTV, manufactured by SONICBlue, offered a feature that skipped commercials altogether. ReplayTV was sued by multiple media companies and went out of business.

While many Silicon Valley engineers sought to impose a computer-centric construct onto TV, TiVo sought to enhance a TV-centric viewer experience. Its TV remote was ergonomically correct; it felt good in your hand. The guide was simple and included thumbs-up and thumbs-down buttons to log viewer preferences, all greeted with a familiar bleep sound. TiVo worked to ensure its design was warm and inviting, overseen by its logo of an offbeat, animated TV character with antennas on its head. TiVo became a cultural phenomenon and, like Google, became a verb. You didn't just record a show; you TiVoed it. The term was added to The Merriam-Webster Dictionary.

TiVo attracted backing from Paul Allen, who invested $3 million, plus a media consortium, including NBC and Discovery Communications, and a $200-million investment by AOL to include TiVo in its AOL TV service, according to *Medium*. It became a favorite plaything for big-name celebrities like Howard Stern, Oprah Winfrey, and, reportedly, Donald Trump. It gained notoriety during the 2004 Super Bowl halftime show when Justin Timberlake exposed Janet

Jackson's breast in a so-called wardrobe malfunction. It was heralded as "the most TiVoed moment in history."

Despite all the buzz, TiVo sales grew slowly; by 2004 it had only 1.4 million subscribers. TiVo was pricey; initial models cost about $400-500 or more, plus a monthly subscription of $9.99. Competition seemed imminent, which could make TiVo a commodity or, worse, obsolete. Service providers started installing DVR capability into their set-top boxes, and the notion of a networked solution, cloud DVR, was looming.

To survive, TiVo's persona transformed from that of a rebel upstart to a supporter of the TV establishment. It transitioned from being a consumer electronics company to one focused on software and services. TiVo befriended the advertising community and supplied it with measurement data. It marketed its OS for inclusion in cable set-top boxes. It staunchly defended its DVR patents, including a drawn-out fight with EchoStar over its DVR device. EchoStar announced that it agreed to settle the suit by paying TiVo $500 million.

The changes were too much for Ramsay. He said he wanted to be an innovator, not a litigator. Ramsay left in 2005. He reflected positively on his TiVo time in a LinkedIn post marking the twenty-fifth launch anniversary of TiVo 1.0. "It's rare, if ever, that you get the chance to contribute to an original idea, execute and be first to market. And have fun along the way! TiVo was certainly the best team effort I have ever experienced and the highlight of my career," he said.

Ramsay was replaced by media veteran Tom Rogers, who as NBC Cable's first president founded CNBC and established MSNBC. Rogers was formerly senior counsel to the House telecommunications subcommittee, where I met him while a Washington reporter. The subcommittee was chaired by Congressman Tim Wirth of Colorado, who played a lead role in cable's deregulation in 1984 and later became a US senator.

TiVo was an early advocate of streaming, noted Rogers, who played a leadership role until Rovi bought TiVo for $1.1 billion in 2016, later becoming part of Xperi. In 2004, TiVo made a deal to stream Netflix, although it didn't materialize until 2008 when Netflix was also carried on Roku, Samsung, LG, and Xbox 360, CNET reported.

"We also were evangelists to the cable industry, telling them what to do to avoid streaming eating their video business," Rogers said. "We went to the cable industry and told them we had the way to combine the cable bundle with streaming services so that the streaming industry would develop with them, not around them. Some small guys understood—the big guys made a huge mistake and rejected those overtures. The course of streaming and cable would have been totally different."

EARLY ON, CABLE VOD SERVICES attracted significant buy rates for hit movies. But overall growth of the category seemed relatively slow. Cable providers were wrestling with the costs of upgrading to digital set-tops and perhaps adding cable modems. They pushed Hollywood studios to provide earlier releases of movies for VOD, with little success. On-demand capability was cool, but there didn't seem to be a rush to embrace it. Or an imminent threat. Until . . .

The concept of using the internet to stream videos was gaining steam. It had a certain inevitability to it. Snippets of streaming's possibility were forecast in multimedia capability, mainly images, games, and audio in PCs and Macs, and by CU-SeeMe, an early online video conferencing program.

In the early 1990s, initial models of cable modems emerged, designed to bring the internet to homes over traditional hybrid-fiber coaxial architecture. The primary focus was on delivering what engineers called data: email, websites, and other internet basics. At that point, slow access speeds, among other things, made video delivery seem unrealistic.

An early peek at online video streaming was offered by Rouzbeh

Yassini-Fard, a visionary technologist who is regarded as the father of the cable modem. His company, LANcity, along with Broadcom, 3Com, and General Instrument/Motorola, was a pioneer in the technologies that led to DOCSIS cable modem specifications. They were eventually awarded a Tech Emmy for their accomplishments. Yassini-Fard told *Light Reading* that LANcity's original cable modem weighed 120 pounds and cost about $18,000 to make.

LANcity presented a demo of video streaming using a cable modem during a cable convention in San Francisco in 1993. The demo showed a video clip of a white dove taking off and landing. Onlookers would be able to see any stutter caused by latency, Yassini-Fard said, but the fluttering bird looked great.

In response, the industry shrugged. "We were questioned by the audience as to why anyone would ever want to do such streaming services when broadcast video works fine and is so cheap," Yassini-Fard recalled. "Times changed!"

LANcity was sold for $56 million, and Yassini-Fard remained focused on streaming. He told me, "In 1996, I founded a company called Arepa that was established to do video streaming over cable using cable modems. Two hundred million dollars later, that company was too early to market, and it died as the market did not accept nor want to accept streaming as a solution."

Prospects for cable-based internet service improved as CableLabs, a Boulder, CO, based R&D consortium, which Malone was instrumental in founding, worked to develop DOCSIS. It stands for *data over cable service interface specification*, but it's known simply as *dock-sis*. DOCSIS comprised a set of specifications to marry cable and internet delivery. CableLabs released DOCSIS 1.0 in 1997 and began to certify cable modems to connect the internet to cable homes. It marked another milestone in cable's evolution, resulting in high-speed internet services and voice over internet protocol (VOIP) telephone service. Triple-play bundles of TV, internet, and phone service sustained cable's subscriber growth and profits for years.

FROM OTHER QUARTERS, EARLY STREAMING efforts began to surface. Former Microsoft executive Ron Glaser founded RealNetworks, perhaps best known for its RealPlayer for streamed media. Since real-time streaming was constrained by slow internet speeds, RealPlayer relied upon progressive downloads of videos, a similar technique used by Apple for its QuickTime Player. RealNetworks engaged in format wars and legal battles against Microsoft and moved into online music while the video streaming market sorted itself out.

TWC conducted an early test of cable modems and IP video with support from RealNetworks in San Diego, according to Louis Williamson. "After Full Service Network and our digital set-top box, we started looking at how we could deliver our video products to another device, the PC, because we had the cable modem there, and it was a screen. If we could get our products there, it was one less box that we had to put in the house," he said in an interview with Leslie Ellis.

But, when it came to streaming channels of IP video, Williamson said, "We just didn't have enough bandwidth. Sometimes you have to put a technology back on the shelf and wait a while for things to get better."

Among those who saw the promise of streaming was Mark Cuban, who joined a webcasting service, Audionet, renamed Broadcast.com, to carry sports feeds, broadcast stations, and other media. In 1999, Yahoo purchased Broadcast.com for $5.7 billion, making Cuban a billionaire. But Yahoo shut it down in 2002, leading *Fortune* to dub Broadcast.com as one of the worst internet acquisitions ever.

Among early streaming services, CinemaNow, founded in 1999, forged partnerships with tech companies and Hollywood studios to offer movies via what was known as download-to-own or electronic sell-through. CinemaNow went through ownership changes, including Sonic Solutions and Best Buy, and eventually shut down in 2017, according to *Cord Cutters News*.

Early efforts around the globe included Hong Kong Telecom,

which attempted to launch a VOD streaming service in Hong Kong in 1998. But it was reportedly doomed by technical issues, high costs, and consumer confusion, according to an account by *Vice*.

Overall, capabilities for streaming video were gradually improving with the growing adoption of MPEG-2 video compression, formats such as Adobe Flash, and increasing internet speeds. Somebody was going to figure this out.

The Hollywood studios themselves (MGM Studios, Paramount Pictures, Sony Pictures Entertainment, Universal Pictures, and Warner Bros.), while keeping a tight rein on cable's VOD pipeline, launched Movielink in 2002. It was an online electronic sell-through service, offering movies and other fare for purchase or rent. Movielink was eventually bought by Blockbuster for $6.6 million, according to a Blockbuster SEC filing. Sony Pictures went on to purchase another early streaming entrant, Crackle, in 2006 and later purchased Crunchyroll, popular with fans of Japanese anime.

If anyone could make the leap to video streaming, surely Blockbuster could. The king of home video stores made several attempts to transition to online distribution, but each took a fateful twist. In 2000 Blockbuster announced a planned VOD service leveraging a high-speed fiber network owned by Enron, a rapidly growing energy company. Enron collapsed amid one of the biggest accounting scandals in US history.

To keep pace with Netflix, Blockbuster launched a DVD-by-mail service called Blockbuster Online and then purchased Movielink, forecasting a possible move into streaming. But the weight of brick-and-mortar stores caused Blockbuster to file for bankruptcy protection in 2010 and start shutting down its stores, removing a cultural icon from the American landscape. The company said it had over 6,500 stores globally, including 4,000 in the US. More than 43 million US households were Blockbuster members. All the stores disappeared save one, a popular tourist destination in Bend, OR, colloquially known as The Last Blockbuster.

CHAPTER 17
FROM THE ASHES

The high expectations of the AOL Time Warner merger were quickly dashed (*Multichannel News*, courtesy of Barco Library, Syndeo Institute at The Cable Center).

JERRY LEVIN'S LIFE HAD REACHED the highest of highs, a career at the top of the most important media company in the world, with all the riches, glitz, and glamour that role provided. And he'd experienced the lowest of lows, an unimaginable family tragedy. But in January 2000, he was back on top, standing arm in arm on stage with AOL cofounder Steve Case to announce a merger that was heralded as the perfect marriage of traditional and new media.

The AOL Time Warner press conference was reminiscent of

Levin's previous triumphs with the FSN press event and the Time Warner-Turner merger: smiling executives, grand aspirations, colorful logo banners, camera flashes, and lots of glad-handing. This time Levin was clean-shaven and tieless, sporting a New Age look.

Some people believed Levin wouldn't have embarked on the risky AOL deal had it not been for the passing of Jonathan. In the book *Tinder Box: HBO's Ruthless Pursuit of New Frontiers*, by James Andrew Miller, Levin said, "My son was born on my birthday. I knew right from the start, the gods were doing something. . . . He was my motivation. All I care about is the death of my son. For somebody not to see that, to this day, it's still my motivation."

Perhaps being back in the hunt, making grand maneuvers and reaching higher helped him to survive the emotional strain. With the AOL deal, he could finally enter the high church in the religion of interactivity. In Greek mythology, after Zeus sentenced Prometheus to eternal torment he was eventually released by Hercules.

But once all the hoopla died down, something didn't feel right. On the front of the building at 75 Rockefeller, above the revolving doors, new signage displayed AOL Time Warner, a moniker that might have even caused Prometheus to scratch his head. Combining old and new media sounded like a good idea until it was put into practice.

Levin had made similar mistakes that doomed FSN. He sped to market and ran through the stop signs. Enamored with AOL's high valuation, Time Warner conducted due diligence for the merger over a single weekend and then Levin announced the deal, with little counsel, the following Monday. Insiders said the strategic thinking about merging with a major online player like AOL had actually been going on inside Time Warner for months. But the end result certainly seemed rushed.

Levin's zeal to combine an interactive platform and Time Warner's content overlooked the fact that AOL's business, built on floppy disks delivered by mail and dial-up modems, needed time to evolve to the high-speed broadband world. Creating a walled garden of content to run on

Time Warner Cable's network of 12 million homes wouldn't be enough to reach scale—again, that word that haunted Levin. (The AOL Time Warner saga is chronicled in several books listed in the bibliography.)

Malone's TCI held a large stake in Time Warner through the Turner acquisition. But not only wasn't Malone counseled about the AOL deal, he was powerless to do much about it. Due to regulatory conditions for federal consent of the Turner purchase, TCI's shares were put into a nonvoting trust. The regulatory bind likely took Malone's dislike for government to a higher level. In the book *Tinder Box*, Malone called AOL-Time Warner "the dumbest deal I ever saw."

While it took a year for the deal to undergo regulatory approvals, Wall Street soon realized that the merger, valued at $350 billion, had little upside. The AOL and Time Warner managers didn't get along, yet another example of how difficult it is to combine different corporate cultures. It was a classic case of the digerati clashing with the old guard, somewhat similar to what the company experienced with SGI in Orlando. According to various accounts, the AOL managers, generally younger and imbued with the fresh excitement of online media, were viewed as arrogant interlopers. Time Warner department managers weren't about to let them control their fiefdoms.

In an incident that was leaked to the press in the fall of 2001, Ted Turner, then vice chairman of the merged company, went on a fist-pounding tirade during a board meeting. He blamed Levin for, among many things, fueling rivalries between divisions and causing the company's stock price to be halved. Levin announced his retirement in December 2001.

A troika of top executives—CEO Dick Parsons, chairman Steve Case, and COO Bob Pittman—tried to keep the careening train on track. But the company had another big problem. AOL Time Warner's interactive advertising wasn't taking off like rosy projections had forecast. The company's financial accounting came under legal scrutiny after it was discovered that the company was propping up its online revenue and subscriber numbers. The SEC took legal actions over the alleged fraud, eventually leading to settlements that later required Time Warner to pay hefty amounts.

By early 2002, AOL Time Warner's stock dropped 75 percent, resulting in a single quarterly loss of nearly $100 billion, the largest in US corporate history. Ted Turner alone lost about $8 billion in stock value, for which he loudly blamed Levin. The AOL Time Warner merger became the poster child for a dot-com downturn that tanked stocks of media companies that had rushed to embrace the internet with little notion of what they were doing.

DIGITAL DISRUPTION CONTINUED TO ATTACK the traditional media industry like a blitzkrieg. While TiVo struck fears in the heart of commercial TV, Armageddon-like worries were raised in Hollywood by BitTorrent, a peer-to-peer file-sharing service that enabled fast transfers of video. For years, Hollywood had been battling to curtail bootleg home video copies of movies. BitTorrent, released in 2001, and emerging video pirate websites threatened to rob Hollywood blind. Just as Napster had upended the music industry, it seemed film and TV entertainment could suffer the same fate.

The industry took legal action to shut down the pirates. Companies invested in antipiracy technologies, including digital rights management (DRM) and watermarking, to protect their content from unauthorized distribution.

Another device that produced both hype and trepidation was the Slingbox. Two San Francisco Giants baseball fans, Blake and Jason Krikorian, created a small device capable of streaming a TV channel from a set-top box over the internet to a laptop. That way, they could watch broadcasts of Giants games while they were traveling abroad. The press loved to recount their story and hailed their ingenuity. Content owners and cable operators fretted about the potential signal piracy that Slingbox-type devices could unleash.

Slingbox offered the unique proposition of being able to watch your favorite TV fare out-of-home, a practice dubbed *placeshifting*. But to do so, the set-top at home had to be turned on and remain tuned to the channel you wanted to watch. If someone at home changed the channel, then your channel changed too, inciting a potential long-distance tug-of-war over what to watch. Since consumers cluttered their homes with devices, chargers, and couplers, most households weren't interested in adding another box to their pile of equipment. Cable operators, despite their initial fears, became some of the biggest buyers of Slingboxes, which they used to remotely monitor channels in distant service areas. Echostar, the parent of Dish Network, acquired Slingbox, and a SlingPlayer app was created for mobile devices (unrelated to Dish's Sling TV streaming service). But as streaming created more on-demand viewing options, the Slingbox became another castoff in the digital dumpster.

JUST AS SATELLITE DELIVERY OF networks inspired many TV novices to get into the cable TV business, the growing prospect of streaming attracted young entrepreneurs, including the founders of YouTube. The three former PayPal work colleagues—Steve Chen, Chad Hurley, and Jawed Karim—sought a way to share videos online in a similar way to digital photo sharing websites. Based on industry lore, the founders each have different versions of the inspiration for the idea, be it a dinner party conversation, interest in creating a video dating service, or the inability to find clips of that infamous 2004 Super Bowl wardrobe malfunction. (For a history of YouTube, see *Like, Comment, Subscribe: Inside YouTube's Chaotic Rise to World Domination*, by Mark Bergen.)

Like other digital pioneers, they had no roadmap. But they had specific goals aimed at overcoming some of the early barriers to website usage. "First, the three creators resolved to create simple software for everyone, including nontechnical people," according to a

VdoCipher account. "They also intended to create a video upload and viewing app that didn't need any special software. They also sought to avoid requiring site users to register to see shared footage. Finally, the creators needed a fast search capability to discover video archives."

YouTube's first clip was "Me at the Zoo," an eighteen-second video of Karim at the San Diego Zoo, uploaded April 24, 2005 (Vimeo, a video-sharing service, had launched five months earlier). Soon, Americans became enamored by what became known as *user generated content* (UGC)—creating your own media and sharing it on the web. Unknown talent like Justin Bieber was given a video performance stage. Suddenly, America was awash in cat videos.

Traditional media was not amused. While the capability to post clips to promote TV shows was becoming apparent, that was outweighed by concerns over rampant piracy and copyright violations. In 2007, Viacom, king of content, filed a $1 billion lawsuit against YouTube for "allowing users to upload and view hundreds of thousands of videos owned by Viacom without permission." That was about $1 billion more than YouTube was making at the time. The case dragged on until YouTube won a court decision, but that was reversed on appeal. Eventually, the two sides settled in 2014.

While file sharing and social media opened a new door for video content, the capability for mass streaming of TV shows and movies at a high quality remained constrained by slow internet speeds and other technicalities. Content licensing and copyright legalities still needed to be sorted out. Consumers needed an easy, affordable, and reliable way to access streamed movies and TV shows.

And so the stars aligned for Netflix.

■ ▶ ▶▶

Despite the AOL Time Warner wreckage, Time Warner Cable came out relatively unscathed. The company continued to upgrade cable systems, digitize channels, add VOD capability, and utilize broadband.

Recognizing the value of on-demand content and recording capability, TWC sought to deploy the first network digital video recorder (NDVR) service, a direct lineage of FSN. It would have capabilities like TiVo, including recording and trick play functionality for live programming. But instead of a hard drive in a box, a user's content would be stored and managed remotely through a headend or other central hub. The service was dubbed Mystro TV. Under Joe Collins's direction, Chiddix served as president, Benya was head of marketing, and Callahan was a principal developer.

The Mystro concept didn't last long, perhaps partly due to skittishness about chasing another expensive, shiny thing, but more because of legal concerns. Intellectual property issues could come into play, potentially pitting the cable company against every television network, movie studio, and ad agency whose copyrighted content flowed through the Mystro service.

TWC stepped aside, and another cable provider, Chuck and Jim Dolan's Cablevision Systems, became the defendant in a lawsuit originally brought by Hollywood studios against Cablevision's similar service, which it called remote storage DVR (RS-DVR). In the comically named *Cartoon Network v. CSC Holdings* decision, a court ruled that it was permissible for subscribers to record copyrighted content for their own DVR fair use, just as it was under the Supreme Court's famous Betamax home video decision in 1984. Cablevision prevailed, and cloud-based DVR services were born.

Now TWC took another lesson from its FSN experience: convenience. With Benya as its front man, TWC, with tech partner BigBand Networks, launched a simple yet effective consumer feature: Start Over, enabling viewers to restart a live TV program that's already in progress. It proved to be popular and won a Tech Emmy. Next, TWC launched Look Back, allowing viewing of shows that were aired during the previous one-to-three days. Other variations were explored, but most became unnecessary once TWC deployed what it called Enhanced DVR service, which provided recording and replay features.

■ ▶ ▶▶

WHILE MEDIA MOGULS PLOTTED THEIR moves in interactive media, a cottage industry of hopeful ITV start-ups sprung up, some of which included former FSN developers. They convened annually at TV of Tomorrow (TVOT) shows in San Francisco, run by journalist Tracy Swedlow, who exhaustively covered the industry in her *ITV Today* newsletter, and her husband Richard Washbourne. Many traveled to International Broadcasting Conventions (IBC) in Amsterdam, where the European ITV market was emerging. Some gathered in an ITV Alliance, run by Ben Mendelson and Allison Dollar.

The list of companies included Alticast, Clearleap, Commerce.TV, enableTV (headed by FSN veteran Tim Wahlers), Ensequence, FourthWall Media, GoldPocket, icueTV, itaas, Navic Networks, NDS Americas, Prasara (with Robert Montgomery and other ex-FSNers), Softel-USA, S&T, Synacor, Tandberg Television, TVWorks, UniSoft, Vidiom Systems, Visible World, Worldgate, Zodiac Interactive, and others. Each introduced various technologies and unique perspectives about what the future of television would be.

Malone's Liberty Media saw some investment opportunities. In 2002 Liberty formed a subsidiary, Liberty Broadband Interactive Television. According to press reports, it paid $185 million in cash and stock for a controlling stake in OpenTV, a middleware and apps provider used by EchoStar's Dish Network and service providers overseas. The Liberty unit bought another ITV software company, ACTV, for an undisclosed amount. Later it announced it paid $100 million for Wink Communications, which created branded interactive TV portals for cable networks and interactive shopping capability. Wink was headed by Maggie Wilderotter, who later served as CEO of Frontier Communications.

Other large players gobbled up some of the start-ups to increase their ITV odds. PowerTV, a Scientific-Atlanta subsidiary that provided as operating system for S-A boxes, bought Prasara. Microsoft acquired advertising software company Navic Networks in a move that was viewed as a larger effort to get into ITV advertising. Ericsson outbid Arris in a $1.4-billion deal for IPTV equipment vendor Tandberg Television, which earlier bought GoldPocket. Cognizant bought itaas, and IBM acquired Clearleap, a provider of cloudbased video services. Comcast bought TV ad-targeting firm Visible World, video publisher thePlatform, and a dynamic ad insertion company, This Technology.

But for most of the smaller companies, the odds of achieving mass deployments in the US were stacked against them. The big MVPDs (multichannel video programming distributor, including cable, satellite, and telco TV providers) took a passing interest in what many of the start-ups had to offer. An occasional market trial or lab test was conducted, and a software purchase might have been made. By and large, the service providers appeared to want to do things themselves and weren't enthused about broad deployments of unproven technologies amid questionable consumer demand for ITV services.

Amid all of the ITV activity, programmers at cable and broadcast networks watched intently from the sidelines, intrigued by the possibility of interactive advertising and opportunities to enhance programming. Over the years, networks offered various features. ABC and ESPN added a so-called two-screen application of enhanced TV features that were available through a website while viewers watched NFL games or *Who Wants to be a Millionaire?* HSN offered a Shop by Remote application for direct purchase of on-air products, which, under HSN EVP of distribution Peter Ruben, gained carriage with Dish Network and other providers. CNN and The Weather Channel developed instant information features. Premium services Showtime and Starz offered interactive guide enhancements.

Yet, for the most part, the major programmers did not actively pursue ITV agendas, and cable providers only supported them with limited deployment. The means to add ITV elements for widespread distribution and handle rights issues were still cloudy and potentially expensive. In theory, programmers could add ITV features to their networks, provide interactive advertising, and seek higher license fees for their gussied-up products. But those interactive features likely would have to be enabled through a cable operator's ITV platform, set-top box, and remote control. That could potentially give negotiators such as Fred Dressler, known for his tough tactics, another bargaining chip to use against programmers.

Instead of ITV, programmers addressed another important agenda: filling the digital shelf space that would be opened in a 500-channel megastore. The biggest programming companies—ABC/ESPN, Viacom, NBC, Discovery, Turner, Fox, and A&E Networks—developed spin-offs of their primary channels to create sister networks. While this expanded choices for consumers, the programmers created network bundles to sell to cable operators. If an operator wanted to carry "the mother ship" network, they'd have to carry the new offspring as well. ESPN, for example, came with ESPN2 and ESPN Classic, and, after Disney acquired ABC/ESPN, Disney channels were included as well. Premium services HBO, Showtime, and Starz/Encore embraced "multiplexing" to create sister networks. HBO, ESPN, and Discovery were among the first to launch HDTV channels as well. Over the years, many consumers got fed up with paying for channels they didn't watch, but the contracts for bundles created a legal barrier to offering networks on an à la carte basis.

There was plenty of interest in ITV, but not enough to entice cable operators to rush to add technologies to deploy it. Perhaps fear would be a motivator.

In 2003, Rupert Murdoch's News Corp. purchased a controlling interest in DIRECTV for $6.6 billion and sought to add ITV elements that would make the satellite service more competitive with cable. Murdoch, who held a controlling stake in British satellite TV service Sky TV, had long harbored interest in US satellite TV. Earlier, he bought his way into PrimeStar, a satellite service started by Malone and other cable operators that was shut down after the Justice Department filed an antitrust suit in 1997, another reason for Malone to hate the government.

In the UK, Murdoch's Sky TV used a red button feature to enable interactive shopping and sports wagering. The planned DIRECTV interactive features included voting for a favorite contestant on Fox's *American Idol*, selecting camera angles on replays of NFL Sunday Ticket games, and getting instant news. Murdoch was also an owner of Gemstar-TV Guide, which developed interactive program guides, and NDS, a maker of smart cards to manage encrypted signals and an aspiring developer of ITV apps. Add to that his ownership of 21st Century Fox, Fox Broadcasting, cable networks, including Fox News and FX, and numerous publications globally. In sum, Murdoch held a powerful combination of content, technology, and distribution.

US cable operators expressed fears of Murdoch's red button as if they were 1950s statesmen fearing the Red Menace of Communism. DIRECTV was growing rapidly, garnering 13 million subscribers by 2004. Its ability to provide interactive features was somewhat constrained because satellite delivery is a one-way technology, and DIRECTV had to use a wired return path to handle interactive responses. But the specter of Murdoch using ITV as a weapon against cable raised prospects that havoc would rain from the sky. The silver lining for the ITV start-ups was that cable operators might be motivated to counter with their own ITV offerings.

"There is no question 2004 will be the biggest year in ITV in the history of the US," Scott Newnam, CEO of GoldPocket Interactive, which created enhanced TV features for programmers, told *Multichannel News*. "Every single operator has moved from: 'We're interested' to 'How fast can we do it?'"

Still, interactive TV was experiencing a hangover from FSN and other bygone projects. ITV had become a pejorative term for some media executives. And the definition kept shifting. Gary Lauder, who often spoke publicly about the state of the business, noted that popular interactive applications such as VOD and interactive program guides, which were originally considered part of ITV, tended to get their own labels, while unsuccessful applications got the ITV tag.

CHAPTER 18
BLIND FAITH

An effort to foster interactive TV through Tru2way TVs proved to be futile (logo and photo by CableLabs).

THE BILLIONS OF DOLLARS AND chest-thumping by moguls and the blind faith of hopeful start-ups weren't going to result in a simple, ubiquitous way for interactive apps to end up on Americans' TV screens. Similar to FSN, their ITV plans weren't going to go anywhere if they lacked a scalable, open platform to create and deploy applications. That word again: scale.

The pathway to deploying ITV services was strewn with

roadblocks. Most of the cable set-top boxes (STBs) that could empower ITV had such limited memory and processing power that not much could be included beyond displaying an electronic program guide. Box capability often varied across a cable providers' footprint. Many MSOs had different models of Motorola or Scientific Atlanta set-tops across their markets. Even if there was capability to run a graphically rich app, such as an interactive game, it would have to be dumbed down to run on the lowest level boxes. It's like when people upgrade to the latest version of an iPhone but their parents are still on an iPhone 8.

Major electronics manufacturers, including Panasonic, Pioneer, Samsung, Sony, and Thomson (née Technicolor), marketed digital STBs to cable operators, with varying degrees of success. Most cable companies and even competing manufacturers were essentially locked into either Motorola or Scientific Atlanta boxes, networking technology, and conditional access systems—the means to allow subscribers to watch cable TV channels. The 1996 Telecommunications Act required the FCC to foster a retail market for cable set-top boxes. In response, regulators sought ways to break the Motorola/S-A set-top box "duopoly," a version of the word monopoly, and create a more competitive market.

Meanwhile, developers of guides and apps had to be careful not to run afoul of Gemstar-TV Guide, which held a vast portfolio of patents on electronic program guide software, TV scheduling information, and interactive navigation (many were obtained through its acquisitions of United Video and StarSight Telecast). Based on a patent search, Gemstar even patented the use of internet data through a TV system. If a company failed to pay adequate license fees to Gemstar or possibly treaded on its intellectual property, Gemstar's cofounder and CEO, Henry C. Yuen, was quick to pounce and file a lawsuit. The industry came to label him as a "patent terrorist," according to *Forbes*.

Overall, the hardware foundation and the software platform for ITV was limited, potentially expensive, and clouded by legal issues.

Cable operators and programmers scratched their heads, wondering whether there was a revenue upside or return on investment in sight. This was not a recipe for success.

WITH INPUT FROM TWC ENGINEERS and others, CableLabs unveiled a potential solution that could encourage mass deployment of ITV. It released specs for a Java-based middleware platform called the OpenCable Application Platform (OCAP, pronounced *O-cap*).

Brilliant in concept, OCAP could resolve two missions. As a first step toward fostering a retail market for cable set-tops, the FCC required that proprietary security functions to enable conditional access had to be separated out of the boxes. That led to the use of a CableCARD that was slipped into an HDTV, DVR, or other cable-connected device to enable cable service—a rather clunky remedy. OCAP middleware, and a related downloadable conditional access system, offered a more elegant software solution. It would make devices "interoperable."

In turn, OCAP, whether inside a TV, set-top box, or other device, would provide a software foundation for ITV apps. A similar Java-based effort was underway in Europe, called Multimedia Home Platform, so that apps could potentially have transatlantic reach. All manner of interactive apps were touted by OCAP proponents: t-commerce, voting and polling, enhanced sports experiences, remote DVR management, and Yellow Pages on TV (Yellow Pages, *haha*).

I wasn't immune to getting caught up in the digital razzle-dazzle. In December 2000, I founded my own business, Interactive TV Works, Inc. It was designed to help companies and industry professionals understand—and deploy—advanced digital services. First, I tried to be a consultant and advise companies about their ITV services. I was a pretty lousy consultant. As clients showed me their creations and vowed that they would change the world, my hype meter was clattering away. But I didn't have the heart to tell them,

"You know, your service has absolutely no chance of success. And I mean no fucking chance." I'd at least offer constructive criticism, but most companies were drinking their own Kool-Aid and didn't want to listen. I think that's still true today.

So I took on the role of an "industry educator," which is a unique role that practically nobody understands. ITV Works published *Advanced Video Product Guides* and *OCAP Primers* to educate the market about the opportunities and players. We held mini conferences and product demos. Mike Hayashi joked that I was probably the only one making money from OCAP. Through CTAM (Cable & Telecommunications Association for Marketers), I taught industry classes for industry newcomers. I wrote columns for *Multichannel News* and technology reports for *Light Reading* and *Heavy Reading*. Later I founded the Interactive Case Competition, a business student case competition, so we could get smart kids to help figure this stuff out.

THE HISTORY OF **OCAP** IS about as topsy-turvy as FSN. OCAP was constrained by competing corporate agendas and unclear economics. Some major media and tech companies with a stake in TV sought to take advantage of the "open" platform in ways that would best benefit themselves. It was questionable whether some players wanted a retail market at all.

Progress on OCAP seemed to be made in 2006 when cable leaders, including Glenn Britt for TWC and leaders of Comcast, Advance/Newhouse, Charter, Cox, and Cablevision, joined consumer electronics manufacturers, including Panasonic, LG Entertainment, and Samsung, at a press conference at CES in Las Vegas. They announced a collaborative effort to add OCAP capability to new digital TVs and cable set-tops.

New OCAP-infused TVs would give consumers the ability to get cable TV without a set-top box and receive ITV apps. OCAP

TVs and set-tops would potentially provide a huge install base for ITV. Subsequently, the OCAP name would be given a new consumer brand name: Tru2way. There was a contemporary logo and branding instructions for manufacturers of Tru2way TVs and set-tops.

Hallelujah! Choice, convenience, and control at last! Not so fast. Either the consumer electronics manufacturers were being diplomatic or downright deceptive. They barely manufactured any Tru2way TV sets. Adding OCAP capability would increase the cost of building their TVs, and creating a user interface would be complicated.

In addition to the expense of developing a UI, the manufacturers likely would have had to license Gemstar's patented guides or avoid inciting its patent lawyers, even though Henry Yuen was no longer part of the company. During a protracted patent legal fight with Scientific-Atlanta, irregularities about Gemstar's accounting came to light. In 2003, the Securities and Exchange Commission filed fraud charges against Yuen and other top Gemstar executives. The next day, the company dismissed Yuen, according to the *Los Angeles Times*.

Instead of Tru2way, manufacturers focused on connecting HDTV sets to home internet services and birthing smart TVs. Each manufacturer created its own walled garden hub for apps, including Netflix, which had built its business on mail delivery of DVDs and announced its subscription streaming service in January 2007. (On a historical note, that was the same month that Steve Jobs introduced the iPhone).

During this time, many consumers contacted me, asking how they could get a Tru2way TV set, thinking that it would give them access to streaming and other online services. It was another sign that what consumers really wanted was internet-connected smart TVs.

Cable operators, who had deployed millions of set-top boxes with limited and vastly dissimilar technical capabilities, faced the expensive notion of replacing their legacy boxes with new OCAP devices. TWC said it initially deployed 2 million boxes and began testing apps. Comcast said it ordered OCAP set-tops from

Panasonic. Still, some suppliers were skeptical over their level of commitment or whether it would be enough to get Tru2way rolling. Other MVPDs appeared to be watching from the sidelines while the return on investment remained uncertain.

By July 2010, Panasonic announced it would no longer sell Tru2way TV sets, according to a Wikipedia history. The FCC threw up its hands, stating, "We are not convinced that the Tru2way solution will assure the development of a commercial retail market as directed by Congress." Instead, it urged adoption of AllVid, a proposal to develop technology to enable "smart broadband-connected video devices" to access the content of MVPDs. AllVid was promoted by an industry alliance that most notably included Google, which joined the quest to conquer TV.

The CE companies began manufacturing smart TVs using various operating systems and connections through Ethernet, HDMI cables, and Wi-Fi. They took a brief detour by attempting to sell 3D TVs. Despite a lot of hype about 3D TV being the next big thing, consumers were ambivalent about wearing 3D glasses while watching TV. For a certain percentage of the population, 3D TV made them feel seasick (a similar issue with early virtual reality). Studios and program producers, having spent huge sums to upgrade for HD productions, were reluctant to embrace 3D, resulting in a lack of content. 4K UHD TV, providing four times the resolution of HD, was constrained similarly, although it became a standard feature in most smart TVs and was supported by Netflix.

With Tru2way stonewalled, the cable industry attempted to utilize a lower-level capability inside set-tops for enhanced TV features like on-screen polling and t-commerce. That technical capability had the arcane acronym EBIF (pronounced *E-bif*, for enhanced binary interchange format). Yet another cable consortium, Canoe Ventures, attempted to use EBIF to enable consumers to order samples or products. But, as with other interactive shopping attempts, the ability to facilitate the transactions and fulfill interactive orders remained elusive. That is until Amazon built the infrastructure to do it on a mass scale online. Canoe turned its attention to providing digital ad insertion technology to enable programmers to include ads in their VOD content.

As ITV struggled to survive, it suffered another indignity that added to its legacy of unfulfilled promises. Steve Jobs, who'd revolutionized computers, music players, and phones, told his biographer, Walter Isaacson, that he had figured out how to make TVs simpler and more elegant.

Isaacson recounted the conversation in his 2011 book, *Steve Jobs*: "'I'd like to create an integrated television set that is completely easy to use,' he told me. 'It would be seamlessly synced with all of your devices and with iCloud.' No longer would users have to fiddle with complex remotes for DVD players and cable channels. 'It will have the simplest user interface you could imagine. I finally cracked it.'"

Jobs died on October 5, 2011, of complications from pancreatic cancer at the too-soon age of fifty-six. Whatever solution he envisioned went to the grave. An Apple TV set with a new interface never materialized. Another prominent tech writer, Walter Mossberg, tweeted later that when Jobs stepped down as CEO "he called me to say he'd remain active on a project to reinvent the TV. He invited me to see it in a few months. He died 6 weeks later."

CHAPTER 19
WHO LOST CHINA?

Netflix disrupted traditional television with hit original series, including *Ozark* (*Ozark*, a Netflix program; photo from 2020 Netflix Symbol Logo Guidance).

WHILE NETFLIX WAS BY NO means the first video streaming service, it was by far the most impactful. Having built a surprisingly healthy service of delivering DVDs by mail, the company was well-positioned to migrate to streaming starting in 2007. Initially branded Watch Now, the service was originally available only to subscribers who were also renting DVDs. It only offered a limited number of hours of streaming based on their subscription plan, and the amount of available titles was fairly small.

In theory, Netflix and the streamers who followed had tremendous advantages over early developers of ITV and VOD, who had to write their own software and toil with limited technical capabilities. The newer wave of streamers could rely upon common software and standard protocols. They could take advantage of digitally encoded movies and programs; frameworks such as HTML5, Java, and Adobe Flash; adaptive bit rates, advanced codecs and caching; cloud computing and global content delivery networks (CDNs); and, most importantly, an increasing install base of broadband-connected homes receiving enough megabits per second for quality online video. Through their online platforms, they could collect vast amounts of user data, the new oil in the media machinery.

The strategy for developing a new video service was different than in the days of FSN, as Ludington noted. "At that point in time, the model was this: Make the technology; then build the business. What you do now is understand the business and find your technological solution. That's how you want to play the game. Back then, we had no technology. We were bringing together disparate industries: cable, computer, and telephone. This stuff wasn't around yet."

The distribution of movies and TV content was set free to travel globally using the over-the-top (OTT) streaming model. No longer was television limited to distribution through broadcast TV stations and local cable systems. It could cross geographical borders, traverse different MVPDs, and extend globally, provided a nation's political strictures didn't get in the way. The OTTs could run freely on broadband providers' wires with no contracts to negotiate or Fred Dresslers to appease.

But anytime television moves to a new distribution system, it's complex and expensive. Streaming required an all-encompassing transformation, much as Levin alluded to about cable's move into the digital realm. Streaming service developers had to sort through video formatting decisions, the creation of interfaces and recommendation engines, and the adoption of subscription and billing systems. To create apps for smartphones, smart TVs, and other devices, they had to take into account multiple operating systems and device formats. The promised concept of "write once, run anywhere" for applications was just a utopian dream. Marketing costs, content development, and movie rights upped the ante.

Additionally, subscription streamers had to win over a young generation that was spending its time freely on Facebook, Instagram, YouTube, and, starting in 2016, TikTok, all while glued to their smartphones, the ultimate convenience device.

Streaming for on-demand consumption was challenging, but streaming of live events, such as soccer matches or other sports, was even trickier. The capability for livestreaming (it became a one-word term) improved with Flash, CDNs, and adaptive bit rates. But low bandwidth speeds often produced buffering and latency issues that left some viewers staring at what became known as *the spinning wheel of death*. Streamers also faced rampant piracy of live sporting events, causing law enforcement to engage in a practice dubbed Whac-A-Mole, a mad scramble to smack down piracy sites as soon as they popped up after a sports broadcast started.

NETFLIX'S DVD BUSINESS ENABLED IT to migrate gradually into streaming, though the tasks were no less daunting. Reed Hastings, cofounder and CEO of Netflix, told *Harvard Business Review*, "Streaming required a completely different business model and infrastructure. We had to build a new technology stack, negotiate new licensing agreements, and educate our customers on the value of streaming."

Diagrams of Netflix's tech stack, available online, show a patchwork quilt of various software for functions, including front end, back end, big data, streaming, mobile, and cloud delivery. To expand its reach globally, Netflix uses Amazon Web Services (AWS) for computing and storage needs, including databases, analytics, recommendation engines, video transcoding, and more—hundreds of functions that in total use more than 100,000 server instances, according to AWS's website. Netflix also built its own CDN, Open Connect, which in effect completes the job of getting content to a TV or device.

When Netflix began its streaming migration, it stood at the gateway of technology's shift toward cloud networking. Ever since FSN's days, engineers debated where the intelligence—the application, memory, and storage—should reside in a network. Was it more efficient and cost-effective to cram all of the intelligence into a box inside a home or to contain it in a central delivery facility like a cable headend or data center? It's a debate about configuring clients, servers, and the network edge that continues to this day.

CD-ROMs, DVDs, DVRs, game consoles, and downloadable PC players had moved the equation to the client devices in the home. With advanced set-tops like the DCT-5000, the cable industry explored using a "thick client" in the home: an uber set-top box with a modem, DVR storage, and other bells and whistles, an ancestor of the FSN HCT. But no matter how advanced, such boxes were prone to become obsolete; a rip-and-replace strategy would be expensive. With increasing internet speed, routing capability, and server storage capacity, service providers could rely heavier upon the network itself, the cloud.

While Netflix executives said their goal all along was to create a streaming service, the original idea was a "Netflix box" that would download movies overnight for viewing the next day, according to Robert Kyncl, who worked at Netflix and YouTube and authored the book *Streampunks: YouTube and the Rebels Remaking Media*. By 2005, Netflix had designed the box and service. But after witnessing how popular streaming services such as YouTube were, despite the lack of high-definition content, the concept of using a hardware device was replaced with plans for a stand-alone streaming service.

Taking it all into account, it's remarkable that Netflix and other streamers made all of the moving parts work seamlessly to instantly deliver millions of streams of on-demand video on a global scale.

■ ▶ ▶▶

As its technology progressed, Netflix addressed the content-is-king equation by ensuring it would have a pipeline of movies to stream. When it built its DVD rental business, Netflix took advantage of a copyright protection known as the *first sale doctrine*.

The doctrine was Netflix's "ace in the hole," veteran tech blogger Timothy B. Lee explained in *Forbes*. "If a studio wasn't willing to license its content to Netflix directly, Netflix simply went out and purchased copies of DVDs at retail. Renting out your legally-purchased copy of a DVD isn't copyright infringement, so there was nothing the studios could do to stop this. And this strengthened Netflix's position at the bargaining table, because they could credibly threaten to walk away from the table if the studios made unreasonable demands."

The doctrine doesn't extend to streaming, so Netflix faced the prospect of having to engage in potentially long and expensive negotiations for each movie it streamed. Netflix needed another way to get flicks.

In 2008 it cut a four-year deal with Starz, the premium service, to stream about 2,500 movies, TV shows, and concerts after they ran on Starz. Netflix reportedly paid $30 million, which seemed like a high amount then but in hindsight was a bargain. The deal included such popular titles as *Spider-Man 3*, *Ratatouille*, *Superbad*, and Academy Award for Best Picture winner *No Country for Old Men*, according to *Broadcasting & Cable*.

Those movies and additional deals for classic films, documentaries, and other fare created a vast library of offerings. Viewers regarded Netflix as the place to go for virtually anything they wanted to see. In three years, Netflix's subscriber base increased from 9.4 million to 23.2 million, according to Digital Trends. By 2011, Netflix became the largest source of internet streaming traffic in North America, accounting for 30 percent of traffic during peak hours. Upon offering a stand-alone streaming plan in 2011, Netflix subscriptions grew from 23.5 million to 221.8 million over a ten-year span.

After paying $30 million for its initial deal, Netflix offered Starz more than $300 million per year to renew their agreement. Starz would no longer feed the beast. According to press reports, talks fell apart over various terms.

"Starz made a terrible deal with Netflix," said Starz CEO Chris Albrecht, who arrived after the 2008 deal was made. During a UBS Media and Communications Conference, press reports quoted him as saying, "You could argue that Netflix built its business on the back of Starz programming for pennies." Albrecht, who was previously a leading executive at HBO, said networks were being "shortsighted" by selling their shows to the streaming giant, adding, "It's hard to turn down the drug, the immediate high of the money that they're paying."

Netflix's valuation continued to soar above traditional media companies, festering growing resentment, even condescension. "It's a little bit like, is the Albanian army going to take over the world?" Time Warner CEO Jeff Bewkes told *The New York Times* in 2010. "I don't think so."

Ironically, Netflix was using the power of on-demand video, which Time Warner pioneered, to beat them at their own game. Following Bewkes's comment, Reed Hastings handed out camouflage berets with an image of the Albanian flag during an internal meeting, according to *It's Not TV: The Spectacular Rise, Revolution, and Future of HBO*, by Felix Gillette and John Koblin. Later, former Turner executive turned media analyst Doug Shapiro posted a photo of a souvenir from a visit to Netflix: mock dog tags that said Albanian Army Foot Soldier.

Netflix came to be regarded as the king of streaming, but it botched its transition from DVDs. In 2011, Netflix unveiled a plan to split its business in two: the Netflix streaming service and the DVD-by-mail service, rebranded as Qwikster. As part of the transition, Netflix raised rates by charging what amounted to a 60 percent price hike for customers who wanted to keep the same services, according to *Time* magazine. Customers revolted, and Netflix's stock fell.

In a message to customers, Hastings said, "I messed up. I owe everyone an explanation." As *Time* noted, he didn't really apologize nor explain the reason for the price increase. But the company was correct to bet on streaming. By 2023, its DVD business dwindled to less than 1 million subscribers and was shut down. Qwikster was relegated to the scrap heap of forgotten brands.

Perhaps Netflix's biggest impact came with its move into original programming. Early popularity of *House of Cards* and *Orange Is the New Black*—each of which was pitched to HBO—demonstrated that streaming would not only be a force in the movie and off-network markets but in first-run programming too. Had Netflix failed with its first originals, it would have been an enormous setback for the streaming business. It would have been regarded as a sign that the new kid on the block didn't have what it takes to offer quality programming like HBO, which each year piled up Emmys and other awards versus its competitors.

Appointment TV viewing was getting overtaken by a new pastime: binging, feasting on every available episode of a series. Soon, Netflix, Prime Video, and Apple TV+ were shaking up the Hollywood establishment by spending big dollars on original productions and winning eyeballs and awards.

Unlike Apple or Amazon, Netflix didn't sell a device platform, but Samsung and other manufacturers added a Netflix button on their smart TV remotes so that consumers could instantly access the service (buttons for Amazon Prime and other services followed). Netflix reportedly paid to get the remote buttons, although it's possible they were part of deals for manufacturers to include the most popular streaming service in their smart TV portals.

Even though it didn't have a device platform, the investment community treated Netflix as a tech company, leading to higher valuations than if it were regarded as a content company. It was lumped in with the overlords of Silicon Valley in the acronym of FAANG: Facebook, Apple, Amazon, Netflix, and Google.

In recent years, stories surfaced of efforts to purchase Netflix before it became a behemoth. Top executives at HBO and Blockbuster each discussed buying Netflix while it was still a DVD business, according to press reports. Wall Street pundits opined that Comcast should purchase Netflix after it abandoned an attempt to purchase Time Warner Cable for $42.5 billion in 2015. Benya told me that after he became head of iN DEMAND in 2010, he suggested that the company offer $2 billion to buy Netflix. But the owners, including Comcast, Charter, and Cox Communications, were distracted by other investment expenses, he said. Publicly, there's no indication that Netflix ever seriously contemplated selling.

To finance its growth and original productions, Netflix borrowed money to such an extent that by 2019, it had about $15 billion in long-term debt, according to *The New York Times*, which noted that the company earned the nickname Debtflix. If it were a traditional media company, Wall Street would've frowned upon such debt and hammered the stock. But in Silicon Valley, irrational exuberance seemed to be the norm.

GOOGLE, MEANWHILE, POSED MULTIPLE THREATS to traditional cable. Speculation swirled for years that Google would start streaming a bundle of TV channels, a prospect that increased in 2006 with its purchase of YouTube for $1.65 billion. With Google's deep pockets, it could absorb the high cost of network license fees. (Similarly, Apple TV-connected devices were released in 2007 and over time offered a full slate of streamed cable networks.) Google took an interim step into streaming with Google Chromecast, a small dongle that enabled internet content to be cast to a TV. It eventually fulfilled its streaming TV aspirations in 2017 by launching YouTube TV, a bundle of streamed TV channels. In 2022, Google paid about $2 billion for YouTube TV to add the NFL Sunday Ticket package of out-of-market football game broadcasts formerly aired on DIRECTV.

In 2010 Google surprised industry observers by announcing it would start a fiber-optic internet network, Google Fiber, offering 1 Gbps internet service for a low price. To choose markets for its initial deployments, Google opened a competitive selection process that led to various attention-getting behaviors. According to a Wikipedia compilation, Topeka, KS, temporarily renamed itself Google; the mayor of Duluth, MN, jokingly proclaimed that every first-born child would be named Google Fiber or Googlette Fiber; and Sarasota, FL, temporarily renamed an island as Google Island. In 2011 Google announced its first site: Kansas City, MO, right in Time Warner Cable's backyard. (Later, Google Fiber became a subsidiary of Google's umbrella company, Alphabet, and was rebranded GFiber.)

Many attempts were made to stream TV channels and bypass the traditional licensing systems of cable networks or retransmission consent compensation for local broadcast TV stations. Some were outright theft, and others claimed various legal rationales, such as Aereo, backed by Barry Diller's IAC Inc. In New York City and Boston, Aereo used small TV antennas and remotely located DVRs to offer an online subscription package of streamed broadcast TV stations and recording capability. Aereo went to great lengths to prove that its service provided individual content for a user's own fair use, not a public performance that required the permission of copyright holders. In a case brought by major broadcast networks, the Supreme Court ruled 6-3 against Aereo, saying it was no different than a cable provider. Aereo shut down, and TiVo said it purchased its assets for $1 million. According to *TechCrunch*, Aereo had raised $97 million in outside funding.

■ ▶ ▶▶

THE BIRTH OF VIDEO STREAMING unleashed a wild child. The television business had been like a classroom of adolescents, seated in neat rows and following the teacher at the blackboard. The kids harbored jealousy toward each other, and occasionally, an eraser got thrown at a classmate. But overall, the students were fairly well behaved. There were rules, structures, and customs over how things got done. Then, in walked a bunch of unruly streamers who turned over a desk or two and finger-painted on the walls. The television kids were jealous, shaking their fingers in scorn at those bad streamer kids. But secretly, they kind of liked it.

How had things gotten to this point? Hollywood and the cable industry could play a blame game over how the dominance of Netflix occurred and the wild child sprouted. The debate could rival a US foreign policy controversy that began in 1949: Who lost China? An argument can be made that Netflix movie streaming wouldn't have soared in popularity had cable VOD been properly nurtured. Cable VOD never became the mass phenomenon that SVOD streaming did.

For years, Hollywood studios didn't provide enough early release windows, so movies were fairly stale by the time they were released on cable VOD. As Netflix grew, several major studios delayed movie releases to Netflix and Redbox, which marketed DVD rentals for $1 a day in store kiosks. The studios (20th Century Studios, Warner Brothers, and Universal) were "furious about a potential cannibalization of DVD sales and a broader price devaluation of their product," according to *The New York Times*. After the studios delayed their movies, Redbox sued them on antitrust grounds. Perhaps to ramp up the pressure, Hollywood urged cable to deploy more VOD services. As a *Multichannel News* headline said, "Studios to Cable: Push VOD."

The studios settled with Redbox, and VOD windows didn't improve markedly. It wasn't until the COVID-19 pandemic, when everyone sheltered at home and movie theaters were shuttered, that some movies were released on a day-and-date basis, meaning VOD distribution in the theatrical release window. But it was a short-lived experiment since Hollywood preferred the economics of theatrical distribution first. When WarnerMedia, then under AT&T ownership, announced in December 2020 that it would release its entire first-run movie slate directly through its nascent HBO Max, Hollywood was aghast. Warner Bros. filmmaker Chris Nolan derisively told *The Hollywood Reporter*, "Some of our industry's biggest filmmakers and most important movie stars went to bed the night before thinking they were working for the greatest movie studio and woke up to find out they were working for the worst streaming service."

For their part, most cable operators didn't sufficiently market movies or educate consumers about the value of VOD (I was part of a short-lived consumer education initiative by Renegade Productions called 4VOD). When added to a customer's cable bill, VOD rentals fueled perceptions that the price of cable TV was too high. Some cable operators were locked into billing systems that were inadequate for handling transactional orders; upgrading a billing system was expensive and complex.

On interactive program guides, VOD services were often relegated to a section that was separate from live TV, essentially existing in their own silo. Early guides didn't provide movie art or much information. Browsing for movies took viewers away from what they were watching—not convenient. DVR recording capability gave consumers the convenience and control they were looking for. Many cable providers added cloud DVR services to their pay-TV bundles to combat churn or offer it for a monthly subscription fee. DVRs provided the ultimate in convenience: the ability to pause live TV and go to the bathroom.

The economics of VOD movies weren't favorable either. Typically, a VOD movie rental fee of $3.95 would get split between the studio and cable operator or other MVPD—the percentages might differ by title, deal, or release window—with a smaller percentage going to a distribution and marketing partner such as Viewer's Choice, later branded as iN DEMAND. Adult movies found their place with certain households but weren't the type of shining example of VOD that cable operators cared to crow about. PPV boxing, wrestling, and other live events often yielded big paydays and typically received more marketing support than movies.

The heart of cable's business was in selling triple-play packages of video, voice, and data. Revenue from VOD and PPV was a sliver on the bottom line. If a revenue injection was needed, it was easier and more profitable to just raise monthly cable rates.

Compared to peddling individual movies, the economics were better for subscription VOD services, such as HBO On Demand. But most cable providers ended up including those for free as an enticement for a premium subscription. An SVOD service with a recurring monthly revenue stream is a better business model than peddling one-off rentals of movies, a lesson that Netflix surely recognized.

"We started running more free TV programming on demand, which I think was a better way to evolve than just movies-on-demand," said Hess, the former Comcast executive. "That was at the beginning of streaming. We probably could have owned that whole marketplace. But we were still cable guys thinking, *Well, I've got a lot of linear channels I can charge as much as I can for*."

Meanwhile, Hollywood and consumer electronics manufacturers sought to preserve their revenue bounty from home video discs. But, echoing an earlier format war between Betamax and VHS tapes, the industry became entangled in a standoff between Blu-ray and HD DVD disc formats, with Blu-ray eventually winning out. A consortium of studios and consumer electronics companies, the Digital Entertainment Content Ecosystem, sought to bolster Blu-ray and DVD sales through UltraViolet, which complemented a physical disc sale with a cloud version that could be stored in a "digital locker" and played on connected devices. Disney launched a competing digital movie locker system called Disney Movies Anywhere.

At its peak, in 2005, annual DVD sales in the US reached $16.3 billion. By 2018, total sales fell to $2.2 billion, according to a CNBC report based upon Nash Information Services and Digital Entertainment Group data. Blu-ray disc sales reached $2.37 billion in 2013, before falling to $1.8 billion in 2018. UltraViolet shut down in 2019.

Between 2011 and 2018, before some of the major streaming brands launched, SVOD streaming revenue in the US alone rose 1,231 percent to $12.9 billion in 2018. Five years later, that annual amount of revenue tripled.

Home video was gutted, cable VOD was shoved aside, and the wild child roared.

CHAPTER 20
THE LEGACY

BASED ON THE LONG ROAD of developments from the first movie shown in Orlando to DVDs and DVRs and then SVOD today, can FSN rightfully claim its status as the birthplace of video streaming?

Some might question that claim. They may note that the cable-based VOD delivery system relied upon a QAM video network, not the web and internet protocols. But bits are bits. No matter how it's accomplished, turning digital content into a stream and delivering it in real time across a network to a user device constitutes streaming.

"This was the first commercial introduction of streaming on-demand video services to thousands of customers," Chiddix said in a recent email. "Fairly risky, very cutting edge, and mercilessly overhyped by various constituencies within Time Warner. But it worked."

A search of technical definitions of streaming often produces this line: "Video streaming is a continuous transmission of video files from a server to a client." That's what FSN did. A standards-setting body, the SMPTE (Society of Motion Picture and Television Engineers) said, "Video streaming refers to the transmission of video content in a continuous flow, where the data is processed and displayed as it arrives." The IEEE (Institute of Electrical and Electronics Engineers) uses the same definition. Many technology organizations and technical papers do go on to cite as examples video transmitted online or over the internet. But the internet wasn't capable of successfully streaming a movie in FSN's day.

Moreover, even before the World Wide Web became popular, the FSN developers were establishing foundations of video streaming that are used for online delivery today: encoding, formatting, storage, client-server networking, unicast, routing, interfaces, and provisioning. Of course, the technologies and methodologies used today are far more advanced than what existed back then. But many of the basic building blocks are similar. It's as if FSN built a Wright brothers-style biplane to hurtle off a sand dune, and then Netflix and other streamers built supersonic jets to travel around a global network of airports.

I spent much of my career as a journalist and researcher, both of which require an unyielding commitment to objectivity. So I had to ask myself, "Was it incorrect to proclaim the Orlando project as the birthplace of video streaming? Was I just saying it because it fit a narrative? Was my judgment biased by personal and professional relationships? Was FSN a breakthrough moment in television or really just a colossal failure that deserved to be swept into the dustbin of history?"

I asked Chris Cookson, whose career in television and film spanned from 1964 to 2014, six decades. He held top technology positions at ABC, CBS, Warner Bros., and Sony, where he was president of Sony Pictures technology. He witnessed every milestone development in television and film, including digital, HDTV, DVDs, 4K UHD, and streaming. When he was at Golden West Broadcasters, owned by Gene Autry, the actor and singer known as the Singing Cowboy, the company provided a movie service using a broadcast TV station in Oklahoma City, OK.

When I told Cookson I was making the argument that FSN was the birthplace of streaming, he politely advised, "I think there are a lot of other people whose feelings would be hurt if the work they were doing wasn't acknowledged."

His point was that, as with any invention, streaming has a lot of mothers and fathers. There was a tremendous amount of development and experimentation going on in various quarters, over many years, using a variety of distribution technologies. The lineage stretches through broadcasting, cable, film, TV production, and the internet.

"I think it was one of the biggest and earliest digital streaming services to actually hit the public," he said of FSN. The real breakthrough for FSN was creating the ability to order, start, and stop a movie so that "it looked like you had a VCR. That was the big deal with Orlando that was different."

For Michael Adams, who was involved in many digital video advancements, the argument for FSN being the first to invent video streaming "does hold water. The main difference is that FSN and Pegasus used a connection-oriented network architecture in which bandwidth for each video and audio stream was reserved for the duration of the VOD session. In the web model, a connectionless approach eventually superseded this, but not for many years—at least ten in most cases—because connectionless IP networks had insufficient bandwidth to provide a reasonable level of service. Remember buffering?"

Beyond the technology, FSN represented a shift in thinking about traditional linear TV. Reflecting on the launch in December 1994, Hess said, "It was a sea-change event that marked the very beginning of the move away from appointment TV viewing."

So if the FSN developers were the first developers of video streaming, could they have patented their technologies and held the intellectual property for the streamers that followed? That's a debate for legal scholars. At the time of FSN, intellectual property rights surrounding interactive media were murky, and they only got murkier with the open internet. Rather than being on the offensive as patent holders, companies like Time Warner Cable were often forced to play defense, guarding against any companies that would potentially claim the cable providers had trod upon their intellectual property.

Nonetheless, TWC successfully applied for nearly two dozen

patents related to FSN developments, according to a search of US Patent and Trademark Office records. Most of the patents (some attributed to TWC and some to parent Time Warner) apply to the inner workings of cable systems and the minutiae of managing ITV and on-demand services. For example, the patents address processing VOD on cable; broadcast applications on-demand; managing media assets with metadata; bit rates in a variable bit rate channel; optimum bandwidth utilization; masking latency in an ITV network; and processing requests for interactive applications.

Nearly a dozen patent applications were filed on December 14, 1995, one year to the day after the FSN launch event. The listings of inventor's names include many of the FSN engineers, including Michael Adams, Ralph Brown, Mike Hayashi, Louis Williamson, Joe Buehl, and, at least for one patent, Jim Ludington and Yvette Kanouff. Most of the patents were granted in 1998, after FSN's time but during a period when tech suppliers and cable systems were upgrading to provide digital, interactive, and on-demand capability. However, there's no evidence that TWC enforced its patents or sought licensing royalties from them.

WITH CABLE OPERATORS AND PROGRAMMERS both facing the growing threat that streaming would cause massive disruption to their businesses, they staged a unique moment of détente. In June 2009, representatives from each camp jointly announced TV Everywhere (TVE), an effort to enable subscribers to access cable TV content delivered online at no extra charge. The announcement was made by Brian Roberts of Comcast and Jeff Bewkes of Time Warner. (Earlier in the year, Time Warner spun off Time Warner Cable into a separate entity, with each company holding its own stock. Time Warner became a purer content company, including the film studio and the HBO and Turner networks.)

Provided that you were a subscriber to your local cable company and were authenticated as such, you could watch programming via apps on broadband-connected devices inside your home. Among the early apps were HBO GO, WatchESPN (née ESPN360), and the TBS networks. Comcast NBCU launched Xfinity Fancast, and NBC Sports used the TVE approach to provide extended Olympics coverage. The industry mantra shifted away from the 500-channel universe of programming tonnage to giving people the ability to watch what they want, when they want, on whatever device they want.

Ultimately, when it came to providing choice, convenience, and control, TVE fell short. On the network apps, most programs were offered after they aired on cable, and the selection of shows was limited. Each cable network app had to be downloaded and authenticated individually. The authentication processes differed and sometimes required repeat sign-ins. TV Everywhere was a misnomer; live programming could only be accessed inside a cable subscriber's home, not everywhere. Inside the home, TVE apps relied on Wi-Fi connections that were often unreliable. The industry heralded TVE as an easier, legal way to access premium content, but critics, such as the advocacy group Free Press, called it an act of collusion.

"The reality is that despite the apparent unanimous support for TVE within the industry, not everyone really wanted it to succeed," said Doug Shapiro, a former executive VP and chief strategy officer for TBS, in *The Mediator* blog. "Some cable operators were ambivalent about supporting programmers' apps and third-party platforms because they preferred to control the customer relationship themselves."

While TVE floundered, cable programmers eyed the growing potential of selling streaming services direct-to-consumer (DTC or D2C). This notion was the equivalent of a third rail issue in politics, a highly charged topic where anyone who touches it might get fried, like touching the electrified bar of a subway track. By bypassing an MVPD and selling services directly to consumers, programmers raised the inevitable question from their distribution partners: "Why am I paying you a license fee for something you're selling directly to my customers?" The negotiators at MVPDs would want their pound of flesh.

Stepping gingerly by the third rail was ESPN, the programming outfit with the highest license fees in the industry. Its largest parent, Disney, purchased BAMTech, a streaming technology company owned by Major League Baseball, in a series of deals totaling $3.8 billion. With that support, the company launched ESPN+ for $4.99 per month, offering features and programming that weren't heavily covered on its cable networks.

Tensions between MVPDs and programmers simmered behind the scenes, but many cable operators came to realize that the popularity of streaming could help fuel their broadband business. The high cost of network license fees caused some MVPDs to wonder whether they should drop their pay TV packages and just offer broadband connections. Pay TV distribution by the large programming groups was shifting from a wholesale model, in which the MVPD was the pampered customer, to a retail model, in which the consumer was king. The mindset of cable providers shifted away from TV, originally their whole reason for being, to broadband.

In 2023, Charter Communications (a.k.a. Spectrum) and Disney ended a dispute over carriage of ESPN and nineteen other Disney-owned networks in what they called a "transformative agreement." In addition to carriage of the traditional networks, Spectrum agreed to offer customers ESPN+, Disney+, Hulu (of which Disney owns a majority stake), and a planned ESPN flagship DTC service. In Doug Shapiro's opinion, the deal "resurrects the idea behind TV Everywhere: Think about linear and streaming holistically, provide pay TV subscribers more value for their dollar, and reduce churn." In effect, the programmer and distributor began treating streaming services like what they are: television.

CHAPTER 21
DOOM AND REDEMPTION

Connected devices and higher broadband speeds provided a viable platform for video streaming (photo courtesy of CTAM Advance Executive Education).

SMART TV SALES GREW THROUGHOUT the 2010s. Smart TVs were part of a wave of connected devices—laptops, iPads, game players, and streaming devices like Apple TV, Amazon Firestick, and Roku—that provided a platform for OTT services.

As streaming took off, the press circled cable TV like buzzards. A headline in *Tech News Today* said, "Why Services Like Hulu and Netflix Are Heralding the Death of Cable TV." Another declared, "The Death of Cable TV Is Coming." *Motley Fool* predicted, "2015:

The Year Cable TV Finally Dies." *The Atlantic* got downright nasty: "The Nightmare of Cable TV Is Over." In marketing promotions, a crop of "skinny bundles" of streamed cable TV networks (also known as virtual MVPDs, or vMVPDs), including Sling TV, DIRECTV Stream (née DIRECTV Now), and YouTube TV, promoted their services as the end of cable TV.

Over its history, cable had been declared dead several times, to be killed off by microwave TV, satellite TV, telcos, and the 1992 Cable Act. The new pronouncements overlooked the fact that people needed broadband internet connections in order to receive streaming services. Comcast and Charter became the largest ISPs in the United States. Cable providers began offering broadband-only plans and focused on the internet speed wars that they were facing with Verizon FiOS, AT&T, and other telcos that sought to replace their inferior DSL connections with fiber-based access.

Connected TV, as it was becoming known, created a paradox for MVPDs. On the one hand, smart TVs and connected devices encouraged the growth of OTT services and cord cutting, thereby reducing their revenue from pay-TV subscriptions and set-top lease fees. On the other hand, CTV helped to increase subscriptions to broadband and freed MVPDs from the cost of carrying pay-TV bundles and supporting set-tops in the home. Early on, Comcast began streaming TV to iPads, a strategy that would become known as BYOD: bring your own device.

Consumers cut the cord in droves, and the number of subscribers for network bundles plummeted. Based upon estimates by the Leichtman Research Group using company reports, from 2016 through 2019, MVPDs—cable, telco, and satellite—collectively lost 12.7 million pay-TV subscribers. During the same four-year, prepandemic span, broadband subscriptions for cable and telcos (not satellite since it lacked broadband capability) rose by 10.4 million subscribers.

The shift in market dynamics raised an economic question that noted financial analyst Craig Moffett introduced in 2007, called the Dumb Pipe Paradox. Was it better for cable to solely serve as a broadband connection rather than be involved in the TV and services that the pipe carries?

Earlier court decisions had upheld the First Amendment rights of cable operators as "editorial speakers." The decisions supported their right to carry The Playboy Channel and other potentially controversial content, even potentially offensive speech on public access channels. The issues surrounding free speech on cable were a precursor to similar debates over monitoring speech on social media.

But being an editorial speaker was proving to be expensive. The debate intensified over whether MVPDs should get out of the pay-TV business and provide only a conduit to the home. There were potential legal ramifications as well, if being a dumb pipe meant cable's status would shift from being an information service to a common carrier. That could open cable to the type of regulation it was fighting to avoid in the debate over net neutrality rules.

In the end, most large MVPDs decided there were strategic advantages to keeping their TV packages, even though they largely had become loss leaders. But many smaller cable operators gave up on pay TV, saying they could no longer afford to offer it. Instead, they referred their customers to YouTube TV and other streaming services or developed their own IPTV package. They focused their attention on providing broadband service. The medium that first brought them to the dance—television—was no longer a good partner.

Cable networks, with their viewers switching to streaming and their MVPD licensing and TV advertising revenue in peril, had to join the streaming wars, despite the expense. The traditional programmers had to engage in a sweeping pivot to embrace the new reality.

Disney's purchase of BAMTech, renamed Disney Streaming, supported its direct-to-consumer services ESPN+ and Disney+. Even with that perceived advantage, Disney spent more than $3 billion to launch Disney+ in 2019, according to the *Los Angeles Times*. Disney+ subscriptions grew rapidly worldwide, generating more than $8 billion in revenue in 2023, but that was offset by the company's plan to spend $14 to 16 billion on streaming content in 2024.

By 2019, more than 60 percent of US households had at least one internet-enabled TV, according to Horowitz Research, headed by veteran researchers Howard Horowitz and Adriana Waterston. The connected TV platform was established just in time for everyone's hunger for entertainment during the COVID-19 pandemic. Cable and telco internet service providers, who don't get enough credit for keeping the internet running during the pandemic, saw their broadband subscriptions soar.

The big tech companies could afford to absorb the cost of streaming since it wasn't their primary source of income. Amazon included a subscription to Amazon Prime Video, originally named Amazon Unbox before going through several rebrands, with its Amazon Prime shipping membership. In addition to producing hits such as *The Marvelous Mrs. Maisel*, Amazon stretched its tentacles into many parts of the video business: sales of VOD movies and third-party SVOD services; Firestick streaming devices; professional sports TV rights in the US and UK; and the 2022 purchase of the MGM studio for $8.45 billion. Amazon's retail rival, Walmart, flirted with streaming, including owning Vudu before selling it to Fandango Media, but CNBC reported that Walmart was concerned about the high cost of original productions.

Apple, like Amazon, had plenty of other revenue sources to lean on as it launched Apple TV+ on November 1, 2019, eleven days before Disney+. During the same period, two other major programmers entered the streaming business by purchasing free ad-supported television services, better known as FAST. In 2019 Viacom purchased Pluto TV for $340 million in cash, and the following year Fox acquired Tubi for $440 million in cash.

For traditional TV programmers, adapting to streaming exacted a heavy toll. A listing by LightShed Partners, based upon company statements, showed the losses by major programming companies in 2022: Disney $4.1 billion, Peacock $2.5 billion, Warner Bros. Discovery $2.1 billion, and Paramount $1.8 billion. In 2022 Netflix posted net income of nearly $4.5 billion, which actually marked a decline before returning to double-digit annual growth.

In what seemed like an understatement, Comcast NBCU's CFO, addressing Peacock's losses, called the migration to streaming "a costly pivot." For about thirty years, programmers had feasted on the twin revenue streams of licensing fees and advertising. The new streaming services were a necessary step to meet consumers' shifting appetites. But it remained to be seen whether streaming revenue could ever replace the amount earned from pay TV.

For many years, I taught Industry 101 courses for CTAM to help industry newcomers better understand the media and tech business. During the late 2010s, we started conducting a media diet survey to probe attendees' changing media consumption as streaming services and connected devices gained popularity. We asked attendees to name the attribute that they first identify with when they think about streaming. I always knew what the first attribute would be. It was usually mentioned right away by seven or eight participants: convenience.

The attendees repeatedly articulated what FSN and other interactive media developers had learned: Convenience wins. Other words that were frequently mentioned: affordable, no ads, original programs, content, binging. During the class, we preached a marketing mantra to the industry professionals: If you think like a consumer, you'll never go wrong.

Streaming services provided consumers with convenience, choice, and control at an affordable price. Their home pages presented graphically rich guides that improved upon the more primitive designs of FSN's Omnio and other early ITV services. They displayed movie posters and TV show images in grids that offered choices by genre and categories. They provided recommendation engines that improved upon the need for search and discovery.

Comcast brought similar improvements to cable with a cloud-based, voice-controlled X1 operating system, which Brian Roberts called "a game changer" for the company. The X1 navigation guide, which Comcast provided through an in-home gateway set-top and some smart TV models, was designed to break down the silos between linear TV, streaming services, VOD, and DVR recordings and make content more easily accessible.

In addition to the business effects, streaming technology changed the way that Comcast and TWC distributed cable networks, VOD, and other content. Instead of using satellites, the providers backhaul cable programming streams across fiber networks to their local service areas. Relying upon internet protocols (IP) for delivery saves more bandwidth, as well as requirements for transmission equipment, building space, and cooling, than traditional QAM delivery systems. Using all-IP delivery, Comcast and TWC, in effect, became their own private-managed cloud networks.

By reducing reliance on satellites—which initially brought them to this party—cable programmers reaped significant cost savings by backhauling their signals through terrestrial fiber networks. All-IP delivery, plus Wi-Fi inside the home, enabled consumers to access video streams on any connected device of their choice, a fulfillment of BYOD. In a nod to the FSN pioneers, this cloud-based approach could poetically be called a "magnificent star-switched system."

The echoes of FSN reverberated throughout these developments: better guides and navigation, more on-demand content, traditional TV, and streaming all on one platform. Yes, choice, convenience, and control at last.

However, in postpandemic years, the media diet answers in my

Industry 101 classes began to change. When we asked class attendees to name the attribute that they first associated with streaming, the word convenience didn't pop up as readily. Some of the other attributes also began to fade, including mentions of affordable, no ads, and binging. Instead, respondents were more likely to name a favorite show, like *Ted Lasso* or *Squid Games*.

Following the initial allure of streaming, many consumers began discovering that it was not the panacea that they were originally attracted to. Faced with challenging financials, streaming services undermined the very attributes that made them popular. They increased subscription rates so that subscribing to several streaming services became as equally expensive as having cable TV. After allowing password sharing to build larger audiences, Netflix, Max, and Disney+ cracked down on the practice, treating part of their fan base like criminals. The ability to binge on every episode of a new series was curtailed since it promoted churn. Recommendation engines appeared to start making program suggestions based more on what a streaming service wanted you to watch rather than what you wanted to watch. Since streaming services operated in their own walled gardens, viewers couldn't quickly surf channels or switch between programs without having to leave one service and sign in to another. Sports rights got divvied up between broadcasting, cable, and streaming, so many live events were hard to find or stuck behind a pay wall. Most of all, people couldn't remember which service airs their favorite shows.

In short, streaming wasn't as convenient or affordable as it started out to be. The result was that churn among SVOD services steadily increased, rising above 6 percent per month in 2023, according to Eshap, run by media guru Evan Shapiro.

SVOD services came up with what they thought was an antidote: add tiers with advertising. As if consumers were begging to see more commercials. The unmentioned deal with the consumer was this: "Hey, if you help us out by sitting through these commercials, we'll shave a bit off your monthly bill. How about it, pal?" At least most services provided a counter of how many ads you had to sit through.

Advertising provided the streamers with a quick new revenue infusion. But so far, the ad community has failed to innovate advertising on streaming platforms by making commercials more interesting or convenient. Despite the overly used example of what ITV shopping would bring, we still can't buy Jennifer Aniston's sweater.

More recently, the industry rallied around the concept of FAST channels, free ad-supported streaming services. FAST services primarily feature classic TV and movies supported by commercials. They harken back to where television began some seventy years ago. Similarly, streaming leaders such as David Zaslav, CEO of Warner Bros. Discovery, advocated that more streaming services be marketed together in bundles. Streaming began to lose its unique proposition and started to look more like . . . cable.

THROUGHOUT ITS HISTORY, TELEVISION HAS been shaped by new technologies that have sparked our imaginations. But imaginations can't outrun technologies' capabilities, business requirements, or the vital need to win over and keep satisfying consumers. When providers of new services and apps fail to keep a laser focus on the consumer and instead chase after the next hyped technology or business scheme, it leads to billions of dollars in losses. The services, programs, and devices that have been successful are those that bond with consumers, truly provide them with convenience, choice, and control, and never let them down.

While the positives of FSN are evident today, the cautionary lessons continue to be overlooked, not just with television but with any emerging technologies. Companies speed to market without having their technology, operations, or business model fully baked. Designers continue to add too many bells and whistles to their creations, forgetting the importance of simplicity. Wealthy egos throw money at the next hot trend with seemingly little regard to whether their bet will pay off. Hype—and outright lying—have led investors and the media to tout the next miraculous invention or unicorn company, only to have it yield dashed expectations or underwhelming results (see: 3DTV, 5G, Internet of Things, cryptocurrency, NFTs, WiMAX, the Segway, Quibi, Theranos, the metaverse, and so many more. What will be the outcome for artificial intelligence?).

EPILOGUE

In Orlando, the FSN NOC and Digital Production Center are long gone. The Home of the 21st Century reportedly fetched $700,000 when it was sold in the late 1990s. The "tired-looking" Sheraton was remodeled. The Copper Rocket Pub was in danger of shutting down, but with the help of a GoFundMe campaign, it managed to survive. Scientific-Atlanta proudly displayed an HCT at its Atlanta-area headquarters, like a college football team showcasing a trophy. The Willards got a big dog that barked at inquisitive strangers, although they still regarded their FSN involvement as a once-in-a-lifetime experience.

In New York, Time Warner moved from its building at Rockefeller Plaza to the gleaming twin-towered Time Warner Center at Columbus Circle. In 2016, Charter Communications bought Time Warner Cable in a deal that it valued at $56.7 billion, excluding debt. That amount was more than three times higher than the Time-Warner merger thirty years earlier, which included media properties in addition to cable systems. The omnipresent Malone ended up owning an estimated 27 percent of Charter through his Liberty Broadband. Charter also made a $10.4 billion purchase of Bright House Networks, previously held under a Time Warner Entertainment–Advance/Newhouse partnership and operated by Bob Miron's progeny, Steve Miron, and Nomi Bergman.

Charter's president, Tom Rutledge, who previously held top positions at TWC and Cablevision Systems, became chairman and CEO of the vastly larger Charter, then the second largest cable TV and broadband provider behind Comcast. Charter rebranded all its cable entities as Spectrum.

With the Charter purchase, the cable company closed its New York City headquarters to move back to Stamford, constructing a shiny glass Spectrum building along I-95. Amid all the moving, the bulk of FSN's history, a formative chapter in digital media, is believed to have ended up in dumpsters. Those who still have an FSN cap, pen, or other tchotchke relish their memento.

In 2018, AT&T, which had sold the former TCI properties to Comcast in 2002, acquired the programming and studio properties of Time Warner for a price that was reported at that time to be $85.4 billion. In announcing the deal, Randall Stephenson, chairman and CEO of AT&T, said the merger was aimed at competing with Netflix and Amazon. AT&T renamed the company WarnerMedia, terminating the Time Warner brand that had dominated media for over three decades.

Only four years later, AT&T, continuing its notoriously poor record of success with media acquisitions, relinquished its ownership of WarnerMedia by spinning it off to Discovery Communications, with AT&T shareholders holding 71 percent of the combined company. Afterward, *New York Times* columnist James B. Stewart calculated that the AT&T–Time Warner deal was actually valued at $109 billion, and it produced a loss of $47 billion for AT&T shareholders. AT&T disputed that figure, saying the deal was valued at $100.3 billion and was "accretive" for shareholders. The merger with Discovery added yet another moniker to the storied media franchise: Warner Bros. Discovery (or as media guru Evan Shapiro calls it, Disco Bros).

After being emblazoned with signage for Time Warner and then AOL Time Warner, the former Time Warner headquarters at Rockefeller Plaza displayed a new name above the golden revolving doors: American Girl. The ground floor of the former home of the world's largest media conglomerate became a high-end store for girls to buy expensive dolls and accessories. It included a café and a salon for girls and their dolls to get matching hairstyles.

Prometheus no longer reached toward a media empire, rather a store for girls. But behind him stood the sixty-six-story building at 30 Rockefeller Plaza, home to another media titan, Comcast NBCU. The golden art deco building façade displays representations of wisdom, light, and sound.

THOSE ARE JUST VESTIGES OF the material world. In the realm of creativity and technological achievement, the pioneers behind FSN went on to become leaders throughout the media and tech industry.

By the early 2000s, Ludington returned to TWC as an advanced technology leader. At TWC's technical operations in Charlotte, NC, he played with on-demand technologies, integration solutions, and ways to squeeze more speed and performance out of broadband pipes. He even got back into construction with the company's 2012 $82 million-dollar National Data Center, a 178,000-square-foot facility that included 1,600 racks of technical equipment and four 12,000-square-foot data halls. That provided plenty of space to play handball, but this time Ludington wouldn't have to do so.

In 2012 Ludington served as chairman of the program committee for SCTE Cable-Tec Expo, the largest annual gathering of cable technicians, held in Orlando. The conference recognized the industry-leading role of FSN, including an article in *Multichannel News*, written by me. Now retired, Ludington lives in North Carolina, where he continued his construction passion with a home remodeling project. He keeps up with former colleagues, most notably by playing guitar and singing with former TWC and Arris employees in a band named More Cowbell.

After FSN, Yvette Kanouff became a leader in on-demand and interactive technologies, first with SeaChange International, which provided servers and other technology for cable VOD; then Cablevision Systems, the Dolans' Long Island–based cable company; and eventually Cisco, where she headed DRM and service provider businesses, including streaming and VOD. Cisco Chairman John Chambers formed JC2 Ventures to support promising tech start-ups, and he added Kanouff as a partner. She and JC2 have helped dozens of start-ups to build their business, attract financing, or get acquired.

Others shepherded ITV services. Chiddix served as chairman and CEO of OpenTV from 2004 to 2007, when the company's ITV platform and media management software gained traction, particularly overseas (eventually, OpenTV was acquired by NAGRA Kudelski Group). Callahan became CTO of Gary Lauder's ActiveVideo, featuring its prophetic CloudTV platform. Levy worked for a series of interactive ventures, including NetChannel, Wink, and RespondTV, before making a career shift to the sleep medicine industry. Each of the ITV services made progress but, for one reason or another, did not reach scale—that word again.

Tom Feige headed TWC's LA and national divisions and, after thirty-three years at the company, moved to online security ventures. He told me, "In my cable career, FSN was the most interesting and fun, as well as the most time-consuming, responsibility. If someone asked me to do it again tomorrow, I'd be ready."

Bob Benya, as a product leader, kept a foot in both the internet and on-demand worlds. He helped lead TWC's rollout of Road Runner, VOD, and features like Start Over. After his years at TWC, he became president and CEO of iN DEMAND, the cable-backed distributor of VOD content, live PPV events, and other fare. He still proudly holds on to his FSN University metallic-covered notebook.

"For me, FSN was not just a career milestone; it was a turning point," Benya said. "I had no way of knowing how much it would test me and push me outside my comfort zone. Each challenge made me more adaptable and resilient, and the constant problem-solving and moments of doubt were all part of the journey.

"What surprised me most was how FSN opened doors I never thought existed. It connected me with incredible people, expanded my skill set, and sparked new passions like Road Runner and more. Beyond professional growth, it changed how I approached life. I was no longer afraid of taking risks, because I learned the reward is often on the other side of uncertainty."

In addition to Road Runner, Rossetti played lead roles moving TWC into telephony and business services. Looking back on FSN, he said, "It was everything streaming is today, without the pizza. To me, what we were trying to do was everything in one app. Now it's multiple apps. FSN was one singular app that tried to do everything. That was tough. There weren't any other apps—we were it."

Post FSN, Mike LaJoie and Mike Hayashi became technology leaders at Time Warner Cable, LaJoie as chief technology officer and Hayashi as head of advanced engineering. The company continued to lead the industry in technology developments, including switched digital video (SDV) technology to route digital fare to individual neighborhoods, for which it was awarded a Tech Emmy Award. Upon their retirements from TWC, the two joined to consult emerging tech ventures.

Among other engineers, Louis Williamson became recognized as cable's father of fiber optics; Michael Adams played lead engineering roles in the development of digital video and multiscreen applications; and Ralph Brown became CTO of CableLabs.

Brown called FSN a "transformative moment" for the industry and said "it marks one of the proudest moments of my professional career. While misunderstood and often maligned by the press, what followed with the Pegasus program and the DOCSIS cable modem became the ultimate realization of TWC's vision for the future of television and beyond."

Others grew personally and professionally too. "FSN was my first adventure in the big leagues and exposed me not just to technical but also management challenges," Adams said. "I was exposed to a much wider range of responsibilities and was lucky enough to work alongside a tremendously experienced and capable team across Time Warner, Silicon Graphics, and Scientific-Atlanta, among others."

Tammy Lindsay moved on to a successful career in corporate communications, often working with Kanouff, including a stint at Cisco as head of global thought leadership. FSN, she said, "was the most exciting job I've ever had. We all worked so hard, and we played hard too. The FSN team became a family, and many of the people who worked with us on this project are still my close friends to this day. We made history and paved the way for interactive television of today and beyond."

The person who started it all, Jerry Levin, opened a holistic center, Moonview Sanctuary, to help a high-end clientele overcome substance abuse and other issues. Later, he was diagnosed with the onset of Parkinson's disease and opened a center to help those in similar circumstances, and their families. Levin died on March 13, 2024, at the age of eighty-four. Virtually every obituary led with the failed AOL Time Warner merger. There were no mentions of FSN.

The last time I talked with Levin, he seemed content, reminiscing about his days in media and enjoying his grandchildren. I informed him that I was writing a book and that, naturally, he needed to be a part of the story. He told me by email, "I never felt it necessary to tell my story, since the development of cable and digital communications came about through the vision and persistence of so many dreamers. . . . That's the way I like to remember those pioneering days. Keep going with your research."

ASSESSMENTS OF "THE FAILED FSN" began to change as more industry players recognized it as the precursor of developments that followed. In 2011 FSN was recognized with an Engineering

Emmy, the Philo T. Farnsworth Award, named after the inventor of TV. The Academy of Television Arts & Sciences cited FSN as "the forerunner to robust video-on-demand and other entertainment and communications services consumers enjoy today."

In a statement showing how memories got confused about what FSN really accomplished, the Academy said, "It was the first service network to offer traditional cable, interactive television, telephone services, and high-speed PC access by integrating them over a fiber-optic and coaxial cable network, which has now become an industry standard." Actually, Time Warner first launched telephone service and high-speed access in markets other than Orlando as the company rolled out its triple play across its footprint. No matter, at least FSN was finally getting recognition.

The Emmy was presented during the Academy's annual awards show at the Renaissance Hotel in Hollywood. But none of the main FSN pioneers were present. Instead, they were in New York for a gala dinner at the Waldorf Astoria to celebrate Mike LaJoie's induction into the Broadcasting + Cable Hall of Fame. They joined together to raise a toast, catch up on each other's lives, and have a good laugh.

Yvette Kanouff was awarded a Lifetime Achievement Emmy Award (photo courtesy of Yvette Kanouff; Emmy Award by National Academy of Television Arts & Sciences).

Kanouff received many accolades for her work in digital technology and streaming, including a Lifetime Achievement Emmy Award in Technology & Engineering. In 2024 she was inducted into the Cable Hall of Fame in New York. She started her acceptance speech by thanking Ludington, who was in the audience. "He didn't just hire me; he sponsored me," she said. She recounted how she attended her first cable industry convention and Ludington told her, "Remember these people; they'll be your lifelong friends."

She needed to lean on those friends after her husband, Denny, with whom she had two children, died. Those friends rallied around her, including sending her flowers every day during the week before her birthday.

"I've made lifetime friends in this industry. Thanks for helping me achieve this honor, for the fun times, the great innovations we accomplished together," she said. "I love inventing new technologies. Every time somebody streams a video, I think, *I had a part in that*. I had so much fun having the opportunity to create things that are now used every day. But I hope we never lose our scrappiness and our hunger to win."

As Kanouff, Ludington, and the other pioneers learned, ultimately, the people were more important than the technology. It was the teamwork, friendships, and shared experiences that led them to succeed. Perhaps even more than the allure of riches, *that* is what drove young innovators to travel to Orlando, Silicon Valley, Denver, or New York, risking it all to take on mountainous challenges. To connect with others, to feel the thrill of achievement, to stand up and be counted. Perhaps that was what Levin was really looking for in his quest for the perfect interactive medium: the camaraderie of people, the exchange of ideas, the spark of creativity, the spirit of the human connection. Maybe that was what was driving me too. Realizing this, there was no need for my hype meter to clatter anymore. This was the real thing.

New technologies will continue to come along that inspire future generations to take television and interactive media to new heights. Those technologies will produce innovations, start-up businesses, and exciting new services. They will also fuel hype, inflated egos, lawsuit fights, and dubious business schemes. They will undergo triumphs and failures. The winners will be the people who successfully work together and do the hard work to find the true value of the technology, develop a workable means to deploy and sustain it, and continue to captivate their users. To do so, tech developers and business leaders need to keep it simple, for the sake of their users and themselves. The fewest clicks wins. In the end, it's not rocket science or brain surgery. It's television.

ACKNOWLEDGMENTS & APPENDIX

THIS BOOK WOULD NOT HAVE been possible without the cooperation and contributions of many people interviewed over the course of many years. Unless otherwise noted, quotes from the participants were made during interviews with me. I'm deeply indebted to all of them for their time, insights, and friendship.

As editor of *Cablevision* magazine, I attended many of the events included in this account, including John Malone's press conference to announce his digital compression strategy; Time Warner's New York press event to announce the FSN plan; the FSN launch event in December 1994; and subsequent tours of FSN facilities. Other accounts of various developments are directly attributed to news publications or books. Many of the news articles cited were found through searches using Wikipedia, Google, ChatGPT, LexisNexis, and my own archives. The Cable Center in Denver, now called the Syndeo Institute at The Cable Center, is an indispensable resource for information, and its oral histories of top executives, all available online, were instrumental in providing background and quotes. The Barco Library at The Cable Center, under director Brian Kenny, provided historical photos and information.

Additional perspective and knowledge about digital technology and interactive media was gleaned through my work at Interactive TV Works, Inc., which I founded in 2000. Over many years, I interviewed and collaborated with industry leaders, corporate executives, technologists, engineers, analysts, journalists, and visionaries—too numerous to count and far too many to thank. Many colleagues helped me to publish guides about emerging technologies, run conferences and panel sessions, and write trend reports for *Light Reading* and *Heavy Reading*. While teaching advanced classes for CTAM and other organizations, I was joined by notable industry co-instructors, including Leslie Ellis, Judi Allen, Sherry Brennan, Sanjay Patel, and Mark Hess. Nomi Bergman and hundreds of other top executives served as judges and mentors for the Interactive Case Competition, the twice-annual business student case study competition that I produce and host. (Learn more at www.interactivetvworks.com.)

The book was expertly edited by Michele Rubin, former literary agent at Writers House, and Miranda Dillon, editor, at Koehler Books. Every effort has been made to create an accurate historical retrospective. But over time, memories become conflated, perspectives differ, and notes appear more illegible. If readers find errors or wish to offer their own perspective or recollections, they are welcome to submit them to comments@interactivetvworks.com.

BIBLIOGRAPHY

WHEREVER POSSIBLE, THIS BOOK CITES facts and commentary from books and publications directly in the text, instead of listing voluminous footnotes. In addition to sourcing material, this is designed to acknowledge with great appreciation the many reporters and authors who have chronicled the industry's history over many years. Unfortunately, disruption from streaming upended many of the trade publications that covered the business; even venerable outlets such as *Multichannel News* and *Broadcasting & Cable* were forced to shut down.

The following presents an alphabetical list of publications, research organizations, and news outlets that served directly or indirectly as information resources for this account (some defunct publications are not included). Following that is a list of books that helped to provide background and perspective. They are good resources for those who wish to learn more about the history of media and tech.

Ad Age	Horowitz Research	Statista
Ars Technica	*Inside Media*	*Streaming Media*
Associated Press	*ITV Today*	*The Atlantic*
Bloomberg	Leichtman Research	*The Denver Post*
Broadcasting & Cable	*Light Reading*	*The Financial Times*
Business Insider	*Los Angeles Times*	*The Mediator*
BusinessWeek	*MediaWeek*	*The New York Times*
Cable World	*Medium*	*The New Yorker*
Cablefax	MoffettNathanson	*The Verge*
Cablevision	*Motley Fool*	*The Wall Street Journal*
CNBC	*Multichannel News*	*The Washington Post*
CNET	*Newsday*	*TheStreet*
CNN	*Newsweek*	*Time*
Cord Cutters News	*Next TV*	*TVNewsCheck*
Deadline	Nielsen Media Research	*TVRev*
eMarketer	nScreenMedia	*USA Today*
Entertainment Weekly	*Orlando Bus. Journal*	*Vanity Fair*
EShap	*Orlando Sentinel*	*Variety*
Fierce Network	Quora	VdoCipher
Forbes	Reuters	*Vice*
Fortune	*Riptide*	*Vox*
Hollywood Reporter	SNL Kagan	*Wired*

BOOKS

Born to Be Wired: Lessons from a Lifetime Transforming Television, Wiring America for the Internet, and Growing Formula One, Discovery, Sirius XM, and the Atlanta Braves, by John Malone, edited by Mark Robichaux (Simon & Schuster, 2025)

The Accidental Network: How a Small Company Sparked a Global Broadband Transformation, by Rouzbeh Yassini-Fard with Stewart Schley (West Virginia University Press, 2025)

Cable Cowboy: John Malone and the Rise of the Modern Cable Business, by Mark Robichaux (John Wiley & Sons, 2002)

Tinder Box: HBO's Ruthless Pursuit of New Frontiers, by James Andrew Miller (Henry Holt and Company, 2021)

Making Connections: Time Warner Cable and the Broadband Revolution (published by Time Warner Cable, Inc. and produced by The History Factory, 2011)

It's Not TV: The Spectacular Rise, Revolution, and Future of HBO, by Felix Gillette and John Koblin (Viking, 2022)

Like, Comment, Subscribe: Inside YouTube's Chaotic Rise to World Domination, by Mark Bergen (Viking, 2022)

That Will Never Work: The Birth of Netflix and the Amazing Life of an Idea, by Marc Randolph (Back Bay Books, 2022)

Streampunks: YouTube and the Rebels Remaking Media, by Robert Kyncl (HarperBusiness, 2017)

Netflix and Streaming Video: The Business of Subscriber-Funded Video on Demand, by Amanda D. Lotz (Polity Press, 2022)

Unscripted: The Epic Battle for a Media Empire and the Redstone Family Legacy, by James B. Stewart and Rachel Abrams (Penguin Books, 2024)

Blue Skies: A History of Cable Television, by Patrick Parsons (Temple University Press, 2008)

There Must Be a Pony in Here Somewhere: The AOL Time Warner Debacle and the Quest for the Digital Future, by Kara Swisher (Crown Business, 2004)

Fools Rush In: Steve Case, Jerry Levin, and the Unmaking of AOL Time Warner, by Nina Munk (HarperBusiness, 2004)

Stealing Time: Steve Case, Jerry Levin, and the Collapse of AOL Time Warner, by Alec Klein (Simon & Schuster, 2003)

Steve Jobs, by Walter Isaacson (Simon & Schuster, 2011)

The New New Thing: A Silicon Valley Story, by Michael Lewis (W.W. Norton & Co., 2000)

Call Me Ted, by Ted Turner and Bill Burke (Grand Central Publishing, 2009)

Relentless: Bill Daniels and the Triumph of Cable TV, by Stephen Singular (James Charlton, 2003)

Bamboozled at the Revolution: How Big Media Lost Billions in the Battle for the Internet, by John Motavalli (Penguin Group, 2002)

Distant Signals, How Cable TV Changed the World of Telecommunications, by Thomas Southwick (Primedia Publishing, 1999)

Interactive TV Standards: A Guide to MHP, OCAP, and JavaTV, by Steven Morris and Anthony Smith-Chaigneau (Focal Press, 2005)

OpenCable Architecture, by Michael Adams (Cisco Systems, 1999)

Modern Cable Television Technology: Video, Voice, and Data Communications, by David Large, Jim Farmer and Walt Ciciora (Morgan Kaufmann, 1998)

Defining Vision: How Broadcasters Lured the Government into Inciting a Revolution in Television, by Joel Brinkley (Harcourt Brace & Company, 1997)

Master of the Game: Steve Ross and the Creation of Time Warner, by Connie Bruck (Simon & Schuster, 1994)

www.ingramcontent.com/pod-product-compliance
Lightning Source LLC
LaVergne TN
LVHW042250070526
838201LV00089B/94